# Lace *and* Ribbons Bows

*35 vintage-inspired projects to make and treasure*

Ann Brownfield and Jane Cassini

## CICO BOOKS
LONDON NEW YORK

Published in 2013 by by CICO Books
An imprint of Ryland Peters & Small Ltd
20–21 Jockey's Fields
London
WC1R 4BW
519 Broadway, 5th Floor
New York
NY 10012

www.cicobooks.com

10 9 8 7 6 5 4 3 2 1

A CIP catalog record for this book is
available from the Library of Congress and
the British Library.

ISBN 978-1-908862-55-6

Printed in China

Stylists: Ann Brownfield and Jane Cassini
Editor: Clare Sayer
Design: Elizabeth Healey
Photography: Caroline Arber
Illustration: Michael Hill

# Contents

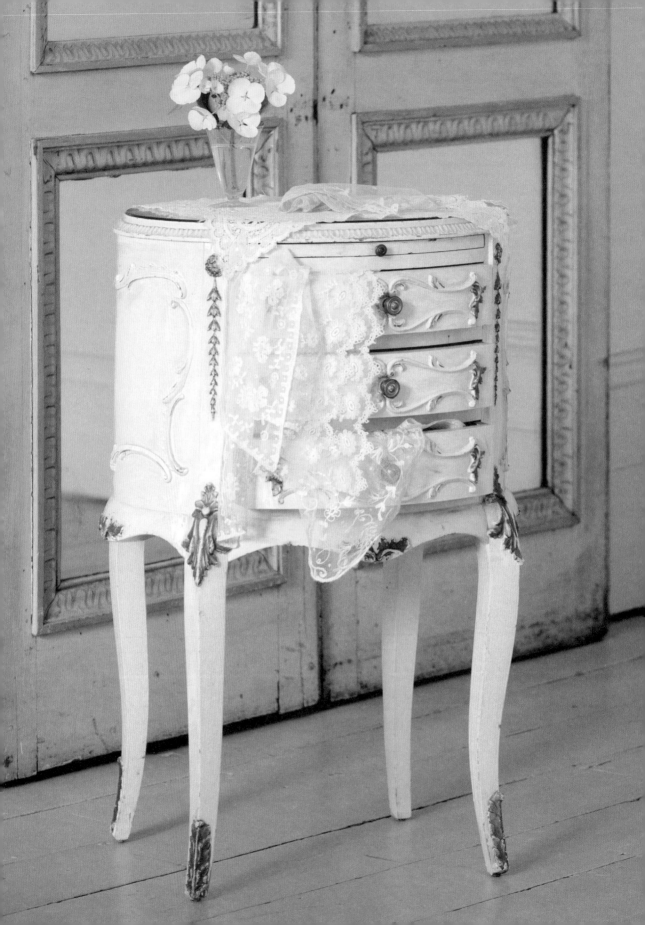

# Introduction

The ideas within this book encompass and combine evocative vintage and antique discoveries with gorgeous contemporary materials to give nostalgia a thoroughly modern edge! A fragment of filigree lace, a dainty doily, a flower-blossom silken scarf, a fine lawn handkerchief, a sepia-tinged page from a fashion magazine... are juxtaposed with pristine new linens, luscious satins and silks, soft wools, and chic ribbons to create a signature style infused with charisma and charm.

The beauty of vintage is how it reflects and adapts with light-hearted ease to whatever ambience you wish—romantic, eclectic, elegant, graphic, or glamorous, with the added allure of imparting a new recycled lease of life and starring role to things that may have been forgotten in the corner of an attic or be languishing in the dressing table drawer, or maybe discarded in a brocante or bric-à-brac stall, waiting to be rescued! Imbued with memory and meaning, vintage will mirror your own personal history, passions, and interests to evoke a very personal touch.

As you browse in flea markets, collectors' fairs, or antique emporiums, you will see a myriad of intriguing items—a jardinière piled high with lace, a basket of silk flowers, a nondescript box holding enchanting old-fashioned spools of ribbons. Neither fragments of grandeur nor modest trifles and trinkets should be missed! The secret is to train your eye to isolate separate pieces, and imagine how these could look in a new

setting within your home. It is the combination of differing eras, fashions, and styles, and the effortless mix of things that mysteriously seem to go together that makes the magic of vintage work. If your serendipitous finds have any inherent imperfections, perhaps a frayed edge, a few loose threads, a small tear, a lost clasp, or faded patina, do not worry, as these are part of their insouciant, whimsical charm. Alternatively, they might be used in such a way that the flaw goes unnoticed.

Your vintage discoveries will come alive by using them in imaginative contexts, and combining them in original ways, with an enticing mix of old and new, of ornate decoration, and refreshing simplicity, so they are transformed into enchanting accessories for your home and captivating gifts and cards. Just remember... your imagination will take you everywhere!

# Alluring Lace

*Lace was once called, in Venice,* punto in aria, *literally translated as "stitches in air," which perfectly evokes its ethereal beauty. Even the names given to various types of lace encapsulate the history and intrigue–Guipure, Valenciennes, Chantilly... Whether it is overlaying another color–delicate or dramatic–or allowing light to filter gently through, lace will always imbue your home with a beguiling charm.*

# Embellished Silk Cushions

AN ANTIQUE COTTON LAWN HANDKERCHIEF WITH ITS INTRICATE lace border, and an elaborate crochet doily, are displayed against silk cushion covers in jewel-like colors with the contrast revealing their fine needlecraft. This idea showcases a modest item, so often tucked away in a drawer—but in this way it can be seen and admired by all! Create a glamorous array of cushions in differing shapes and shades, with or without a flange, each fastened at the back with a slender silk loop, slipped over the daintiest mother-of-pearl vintage buttons. In this way, both sides of the cushions are equally pretty.

**SEE PAGE 88** FOR INSTRUCTIONS

# Silk *and* Lace Bolster

A TREASURED HEIRLOOM OF INTRICATE ANTIQUE LACE, originally designed to grace a dressing table, makes an enchanting decoration for a softly swathed silk bolster, and will complement a pretty chair, chaise longue, or day bed. Reminiscent of a past romantic era, the bolster is loosely gathered and secured at each end by ties of matching silk, tied into voluptuous bows. As an alternative, delicate vintage ribbon or braid—perhaps found in a bric-à-brac stall—could be used instead. Shimmering mismatched mother-of-pearl buttons secure the back of the bolster and give a beautiful finishing touch.

SEE PAGE 90 FOR INSTRUCTIONS

# Silk Satin Pouches

COTTON LACE AND CROCHET PLACEMATS FROM A PAST ERA take on new roles as romantic decorations for silk satin pouches—so useful for safely hiding mementoes and keepsakes or storing pretty gloves and pearls. These simple envelope-shaped pouches are sewn from soft satin which can be found in the most glorious colors such as chartreuse, rose pink, vanilla, amethyst, and aquamarine. Each has slender satin ties, and the extra embellishment of a fragile pearlized buckle or a dramatic iridescent brooch will ensure that this becomes the loveliest addition to your dressing table or boudoir.

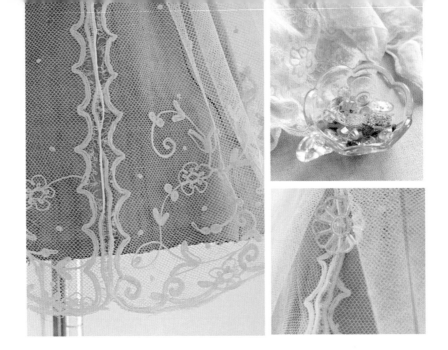

# Frou-frou Lampshade

THIS ETHEREAL SHADE IS CREATED BY MAKING AN underskirt of silvery-gray silk dupion that is then overlaid with fragile embroidered tulle and it would perfectly complement a beautiful vintage glass lamp stand. The light filtering between the two gently gathered layers enhances the intricate embroidery of the lace panel. The lace was originally part of a 1950s christening gown, to be found and rescued from a street market stall and given a new role. A collection of tiny antique glass buttons, or a single statement button, sewn to catch the scalloped edges, will refract the light whilst imbuing a soft romantic ambience.

SEE PAGE 94 FOR INSTRUCTIONS

# Filigree Curtain

A COLLECTION OF DELIGHTFUL LACE AND CROCHET doily placemats are suddenly irresistible instead of old-fashioned! Each is lightly stitched on to a length of sheer cotton voile to form a random, undulating band within the center section of the voile. The daylight filtering through each design creates ethereal silhouettes—reminiscent of snowflakes, flowers, or kaleidoscopic patterns—encapsulating the beauty of these crafts, in a graphic way. Perhaps for a child's room you could try dyeing each doily in pastel shades for a pretty look, or in primary colors for more impact.

**SEE PAGE 96** FOR INSTRUCTIONS

# Lace *and* Burmese Cotton Runner

THIS TABLE RUNNER, SO SIMPLE AND EASY TO MAKE, has a subtle, rustic charm. A panel of fine antique lace, with its intricate flower detailing and pretty edging, overlays a length of raw Burmese cotton, creating a contrast between the delicate and homespun textures. Lace panels such as this are sometimes handed down as heirlooms and often placed in the back of a drawer and forgotten, so this is a lovely way to reveal its quiet beauty in your home. The runner can be used on its own, or placed over a heavy linen tablecloth, to give a soft, layered effect.

SEE PAGE 97 FOR INSTRUCTIONS

# Doily Corsage Napkins

INTRICATE DOILIES—OLD-FASHIONED, ORNAMENTAL placemats—were crocheted or knitted in an array of differing, openwork patterns out of cotton or linen thread, starting from the center and working outward. Their heyday was during the early twentieth century, when pattern books were produced showcasing different designs, from the simple to the ornate, but today their simple charm still beguiles! Doilies are the perfect size and shape to fold into the sweetest, corsage flowers. With discreet stems and ribbon ties to hold the napkins in place, they will decorate and enhance a pretty table setting. When your guests have left, just arrange them in a delicate glass vase encircled with the ribbon.

SEE PAGE 98 FOR INSTRUCTIONS

# Tissue *and* Lace Gift Bags

EXQUISITE WRAPPING MAKES THE SIMPLEST OF GIFTS alluring, and these translucent gift bags show the intricate beauty of lace—the most romantic and evocative of textiles—to stunning effect. However, they are so simple to make and are surprisingly strong as the tissue lining lends support to the delicate fabric. Just combine the prettiest colored tissue paper you can find with ivory, milk-white or cream lace. Fill with bonbons, amaretti biscuits rustling in their tissue wraps, or fragrant soaps. The gift may be transient but these gift bags will be treasured forever.

**SEE PAGE 99** FOR INSTRUCTIONS

# Lace Jewelry Roll

LACE, ONCE CONSIDERED MORE PRECIOUS THAN gemstones, is perfect for this glamorous, feminine, *and* functional jewelry roll—a safe haven for your collection of necklaces, earrings, brooches, and rings. Made from sophisticated slubbed dupion silk and a piece of delicate antique lace, there are three small pockets, and a larger one with a slender zipper, as well as a soft velvet ribbon to hold your rings, secured at the end with a tiny button. The roll is gently folded over so the lace overlay is apparent, to become a gorgeous accessory for the dressing table or bedroom. Just pin a vintage brooch to the front for an additional *je ne sais quoi*.

SEE PAGE 100 FOR INSTRUCTIONS

# Lace *and* Ribbon Tie-backs

A DRAMATIC LACE AND RIBBON tie-back for a luxurious silk curtain is created from the simplest of materials—a piece of unusual *café-au-lait* lace, sourced while browsing in a French flea market, and a length of wide, somberly-colored antique silk ribbon. The addition of a nineteenth-century paste clasp adds to the romantic *Belle Epoque* atmosphere. If you need two tie-backs for a pair of curtains, use the same or similar ribbon, and just choose another lace piece that complements to achieve an eclectic *vive la différence* look!

SEE PAGE 102 FOR INSTRUCTIONS

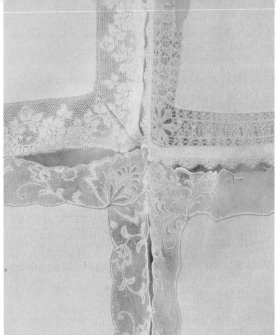

# Handkerchief
## Café Curtain

A COLLECTION OF FINE LAWN VINTAGE HANKIES, trimmed with lace and embroidery, are starched and stitched to become a charming café curtain, ensuring privacy whilst both diffusing the light and creating a calm, harmonious atmosphere. Venetian ladies in the sixteenth century would carry a square of pure flax or *lanolawn*—decorated with beautiful lace to signify style and wealth—and the way these handkerchiefs were worn or used, conveyed different meanings or messages. By using these vintage items in your home you can rediscover the simple pleasures of the past.

SEE PAGE 103 FOR INSTRUCTIONS

# Handkerchief Envelopes

TAKING INSPIRATION FROM THE SIMPLE SHAPE OF THE ordinary paper envelope, these ethereal lace-embellished envelopes are so inviting! Each hankie is folded and sewn to contain a "thank you" card, with the message created from individual letters cut from contemporary magazines, using an eclectic mélange of typefaces in gentle colors. Just arrange the letters in an informal fashion on a smooth ivory paper to achieve a graphic design. The addition of an iridescent vintage button sewn to each hankie becomes the full point!

SEE PAGE 104 FOR INSTRUCTIONS

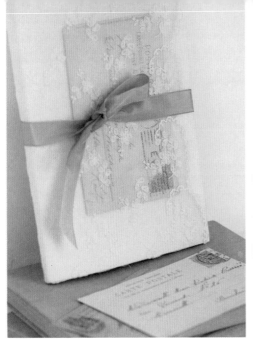

# Nostalgia Notebook

AN ORDINARY NOTEBOOK IS GIVEN THE "CINDERELLA" treatment, and transformed with a lace-sheathed cover into an enchanting journal. One prettily-edged side is left open, into which you can slip a vintage picture postcard, to display either the nostalgic image, or the graceful pen and ink handwriting and intriguing postmark, evocative of a past era. Simply gather your keepsakes—a rail or theater ticket, an elegant hotel letterhead, a café menu card—any mementoes or ephemera that evoke happy memories of holidays and celebrations, and display them inside the pages.

SEE PAGE 105 FOR INSTRUCTIONS

# Arrays *of* Ribbons

*The simplicity and charm of ribbon to adorn and decorate has
captured the imagination throughout the eras. Today a chance
brocante or flea-market discovery—a spool of slender silk ribbon,
a fragment of gilded metallic braid, or perhaps contemporary
grosgrains and velvets in delicious hues—will all continue
to enthrall.*

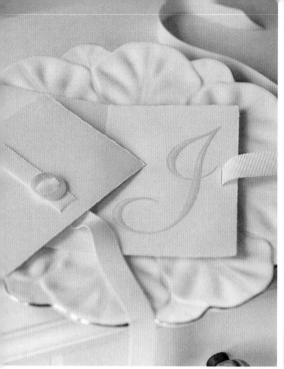

# Rose *and* Concertina Cards

THESE ENDEARING HAND-PAINTED CARDS ARE SIMPLICITY itself. A nostalgic mélange of a 1950s-inspired rose floral motif, swirling swash capital letters, and shimmering vintage mother-of-pearl buckles encapsulates the mood of summer. You could choose a different flower if you prefer—try bluebells or tulips, or, for a winter greeting card, why not a snowdrop or hellebore—let your creativity blossom! Alternatively, a beautifully inscribed initial letter, painted in pretty pastel colors, can inspire a concertina card. The picturesque imagery is enhanced with slender grosgrain ribbons, either encircling a painted stem or threaded through delicate buckles. This collection is the season's debut of the prettiest greeting cards!

SEE PAGE 106–108 FOR INSTRUCTIONS

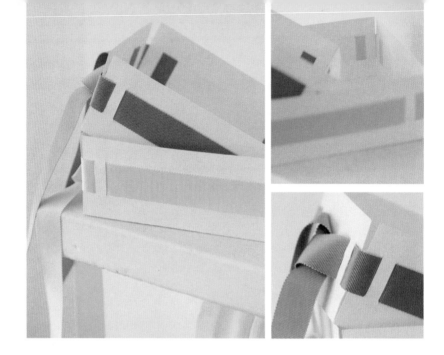

# Slotted Ribbon Box

THE SWEETEST GIFT BOX OF THE SEASON CAN BE fashioned from luxurious ivory watercolor paper and pretty pastel-colored grosgrain ribbon that is threaded through neatly cut slits. This simple threading and slotting technique enables each box to hold its shape firmly whilst giving a chic tailored effect, and the "couture" look can be adjusted according to the number and position of each cut. If you wish, add an extra dimension by lining the box with a layer of translucent glassine paper, folded over, just to give a tantalizing glimpse of the gift within.

**SEE PAGE 109** FOR INSTRUCTIONS

# Beribboned Tags

SLENDER RIBBONS IN SUGAR-CANDY COLORS ARE threaded through homemade gift tags, decorated with a hand-painted rose or rosebud, swirling calligraphic letters or numerals in soft toning shades. Images from a bygone era and nostalgic typography can be easily found in pretty postcards from the Victorian and Edwardian eras, as well as in vintage fashion and dressmaking magazines and in childrens' picture books or illustrated botany books. Browse in antiquarian or secondhand bookshops and bric-à-brac stalls for inspiration to suit a specific anniversary or celebration, and then create the sweetest tags for special gifts to delight the recipients!

**SEE PAGE 110** FOR INSTRUCTIONS

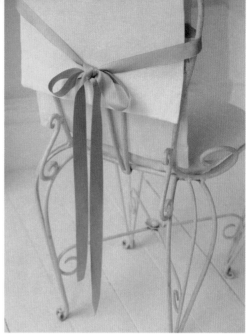

# Vintage Scarf Chairbacks

SILK FLORAL SCARVES FROM THE 1950S ARE AN ENCHANTING source of inspiration, as the eclectic patterns and colors are rarely reproduced in contemporary fabrics and the designs convey an elusive sense of the past. This scarf, with its soft pattern of blossoms, has been cut into panels and combined with soft, white linen to make pretty chairbacks—perfect for when you want to unify a collection of different chairs. Tied at the back with loose bows of toning shades of ribbon, they create a lovely effect. Make for a special celebration, a garden party, or simply to add charm to a favorite seat.

SEE PAGE 112 FOR INSTRUCTIONS

# Jeweled Mirror

A JUNK MIRROR—DISCARDED, DAMAGED, AND BEREFT of its frame—is salvaged and revamped as a sparkling ornament for a mantelpiece or console table. Vintage diamanté brooches and buckles—even a solitary earring—can be used for decorative effect, to enhance reflection and radiance. There's no need to worry if any are broken, such as a lost clip or missing clasp, as this will not show. In the past, lustrous metallic ribbons were often used as embellishment to religious robes or ceremonial gowns and were woven in shimmering gold, silver, and bronze threads. When folded into a loop, the ribbon will retain its upright shape to adorn your unique mirror.

SEE PAGE 113 FOR INSTRUCTIONS

# Vintage
## Drawstring Bags

A SMALL PIECE OF PRINTED COTTON FEATURING a quaint, naive farmyard motif, with graphic black outlines and sweeps of color in yellow, turquoise, and mauve, epitomizes the quirky textile designs of the 1950s and 1960s. If you find a quixotically patterned fabric, even just a small amount, it makes sense to combine it with a contemporary material whilst retaining it as the key feature. These adorable bags each have a useful pocket to store buttons, or whatever else you wish, and a homemade "ribbon" to act as the drawstring, both sewn from the vintage fabric.

SEE PAGE 114 FOR INSTRUCTIONS

# Blossom *and* Fern Tie Cushion

ADD A NONCHALANT FEEL TO AN IVORY LINEN CUSHION... as the back becomes the front! Pretty printed ties showing blossoms, leaves, and ferns are created from a vintage scarf to secure the opening—such a simple idea, yet it evokes a relaxed, bohemian look. The back of the cushion is not left out, but has a bijou patch, also cut from the scarf to unify the design. Flower and leaf designs were key motifs for scarves of the 1940s and 1950s, so are perfect to add to a cushion to place on a 1950s garden chair, with the rich tones of the scarf picking up the beautiful patina of the wrought ironwork.

SEE PAGE 116 FOR INSTRUCTIONS

# Velvet Ribbon Throw

REMINISCENT OF INTERIORS FURNISHINGS in turn-of-the-century country homes, this luxurious throw is sewn from the softest wool, with its natural selvedge, and decorated with shimmering velvet ribbon and a flamboyant chiffon-petaled flower. Velvet is a delight to the senses—the fabric most probably originated in Italy and would have been woven from silk from the Far East, and used as cloth and embellishments for the rich and noble. Now velvet is more likely to be made from rayon and other fibers but, nevertheless, the sensuous pile still catches the light to dramatic effect.

SEE PAGE 118 FOR INSTRUCTIONS

# Rosette Frame

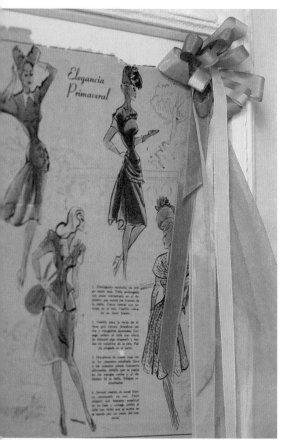

A NOSTALGIC ILLUSTRATION, FOUND torn from a 1940s Spanish fashion magazine, is given new life and impact within a carved wooden frame, and enhanced with a stream of slender ribbons. The ribbons, caught into a rosette, and with their faded hues of sepia, pink, and coral, have been chosen to match the gentle colors of the image. Remember to retain any torn, worn, or discolored edges of the page, as these are part of the mystique, and add to its poignant beauty. Old wooden frames can still be picked up at bargain prices and simply updated with a coat of paint—just choose a pretty color to complement your vintage image.

SEE PAGE 119 FOR INSTRUCTIONS

# A La Mode Cards

THE SIMPLICITY OF SLENDER RIBBONS encircling chic monochrome images taken from vintage fashion magazines is understated and elegant. Each is pinned with a glittering vintage bouquet brooch of the 1940s or 1950s, and decorated with an embroidered label, similar to the utilitarian nametags sewn into school uniforms. This stylish collection of items, placed together on a textured ivory watercolor paper, becomes an elegant greeting card and a little gift. Line each with translucent tracing or glassine paper to create inner pages and create an air of "couture" luxury.

SEE PAGE 120 FOR INSTRUCTIONS

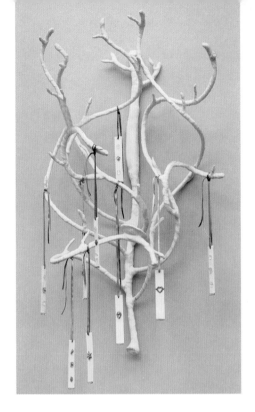

# Diamanté Pendants

A TREASURE TROVE OF GLISTENING TRINKETS, GLASS BUTTONS, and other serendipitous bric-à-brac finds are placed on slender rectangles of pure white watercolor paper, either in groups of three or as a single sparkling piece, to create a collection of decorations that are transformed into enchanting heirloom treasures! Delicate ribbons in somber hues of stormy gray, aquamarine, and turquoise are threaded through the pendants which, when gathered together, form an ethereal display—perhaps suspended from a white wintry branch or a chandelier? Individually, they become a glittering gift tag or token.

SEE PAGE 121 FOR INSTRUCTIONS

# Beautiful Bows

*The bow—such an enchanting accessory or embellishment, formed by the simplest twist and loop. It can be created from ribbon, satin, raffia… but will always add that certain* joie de vivre. *Whether chic and tailored, or sumptuous and graceful, the bow imparts a most feminine style.*

# Raffia Lampshade

REMINISCENT OF SUMMER HOLIDAYS AND STRAW HATS, this raffia shade will bring back happy memories! The traditional craft of raffia work is adapted by wrapping long strands of natural raffia around a wire lamp frame, to create a charming and rustic effect, whilst allowing the light to filter through the raffia. An oversized bow of burlap (hessian) hat trim adds a fashionable dimension when placed at a jaunty angle. Or perhaps, choose a gaily striped vintage silk fabric or ribbon, folded into an exuberant bow to add the final flourish.

SEE PAGE 122 FOR INSTRUCTIONS

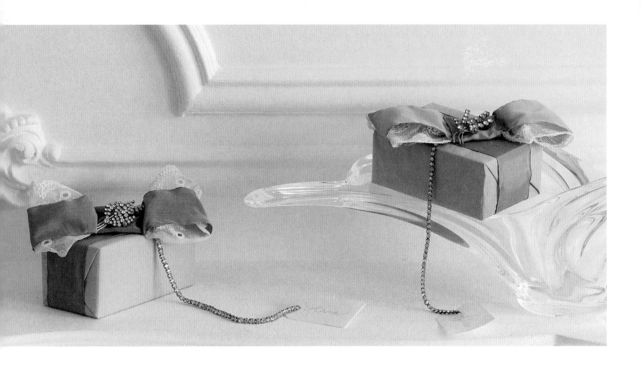

# Diamanté Gift Wraps

PALEST TAUPE TISSUE PAPER IS USED TO ENCASE GIFT BOXES—
the delicate color a perfect foil for either an intense-hued wired ribbon
in an iridescent turquoise, or alternatively a subtle *café-au-lait* shade.
Each ribbon has a froth of lace as an underlayer to give an extra-pretty
effect. Inexpensive bric-à-brac finds of vintage diamanté brooches in
spray and bouquet designs, so quintessential to the fashion of the 1950s,
are pinned to the center of each voluptuous bow, to catch the light.
Lastly, a fragile strand of diamanté, together with a handwritten label, is
added to each little parcel to give a certain indefinable sparkle.

**SEE PAGE 123** FOR INSTRUCTIONS

# Floral Linen Runner

TAKE INSPIRATION FROM A LENGTH OF VINTAGE DRESS fabric in a fresh cotton print, the colors and pattern evocative of summers past. From dainty florals to rainwashed blooms, the designs for dress materials of the 1940s through to the 1960s are pure delight, and conjure up all sorts of possibilities. Combine your choice of pattern with the softest slubbed linen, in a toning shade, to create a runner for your dining or console table. The addition of chic grosgrain ribbon, sewn along the joining seams, with matching tailored bows, makes this runner reminiscent of the timeless fashion of the fifties... from frocks to your home !

SEE PAGE 124 FOR INSTRUCTIONS

# Napkins *with*
# Bow Holders

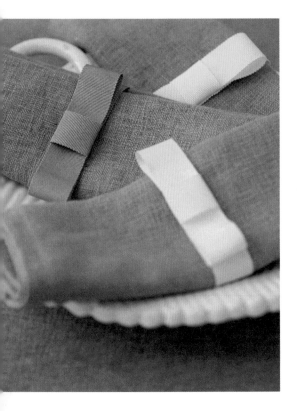

MATCHING NAPKINS ARE AN ELEGANT addition to a homemade tablecloth or runner, and a useful way to use any leftover fabric. These soft linen napkins have holders made from grosgrain ribbon, which you can find in a rainbow palette of colors, from pretty pastels to vivid citrus shades, as well as muted grays and navy blues. Grosgrain has a distinctive ribbed weave, and with its matte or subtle luster finish, it adds panache to any project, so is perfect for these chic little bows. To add a final finishing touch, decorate each ribbon with a little vintage 1950s button.

SEE PAGE 126 FOR INSTRUCTIONS

## *Ooh La La*
# Lampshade

THIS WHIMSICAL AND ALLURING SHADE ADDS A light-hearted sophistication to your home and will showcase a 1950s vintage scarf, with its elegant, floral motif and unusual coloring, to wonderful advantage. The fashion for scarves in the 1950s through to the 1970s can be a real source of inspiration. It is a delight to wander through secondhand stores or bric-à-brac markets to discover a silk or rayon scarf that has the potential to fulfill a new starring role. Just add a beautiful bow and a swathe of translucent tulle and voilà—a lampshade that epitomizes glamour!

SEE PAGE 128 FOR INSTRUCTIONS

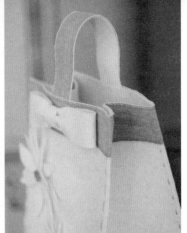

# Daisy Handbag

EVOKE A LADYLIKE 1950S STYLE—PRIM BUT NOT AT ALL proper! Cut and hand stitched from soft felt, this handbag has a subtle contrasting trim and a handle of open-weave braid. Extra embellishments of adorable double-petal felt daisies, complete with sparkling glass button centers and a 1950s felt bow, encapsulate the ultimate femininity of this era. Felt comes in an array of colors, so perhaps try blush or lipstick pink, or powder blue? This handbag is the ideal size to hold a silk scarf, a pair of gloves, and a vintage compact.

SEE PAGE 130 FOR INSTRUCTIONS

# Summer Straw Basket

A PRETTY SUNDRESS AND SUNHAT WITH A STRAW BASKET swinging on your arm... this pretty bag conjures up dreamy summer days. An enchanting basket can be created from a treasured, unworn, or vintage straw hat and decorated with a chic, pristine white double bow in that most quintessentially summery fabric—broderie anglaise. This cutout and white-work technique probably originated in the ninth century in Czechoslovakia and has always been popular but re-emerged as an iconic fabric when Brigitte Bardot wore a wedding dress of gingham trimmed with broderie anglaise.

SEE PAGE 134 FOR INSTRUCTIONS

# Lingerie Envelope

THIS DUSKY ROSE SILK LINGERIE ENVELOPE IS LINED with a 1960s Parisian souvenir scarf, printed with iconic motifs of the Eiffel Tower, Notre Dame, Sacré Coeur, and the Arc de Triomphe. It is unmistakeably imbued with the nostalgia of travel, honeymoons, and, of course, with the romantic movies of the 1950s and 1960s. Complete the picture with a voluptuous silk bow and a beautiful button, and store your delicate camisoles or negligées within. Just adapt this idea with a scarf from your own travels, and choose a silk to blend with your personal color scheme.

  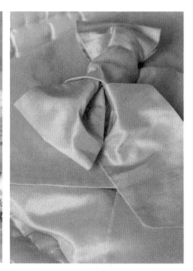

SEE PAGE 132 FOR INSTRUCTIONS

# Needlework Case

AN ESSENTIAL ACCESSORY FOR every seamstress! This is stylish and functional, made from soft wool and a contrasting colored lining. It has a useful pocket, a booklet for pins and needles, and inserts to store other sewing paraphernalia, such as hooks and eyes, snap fasteners (press studs,) and a tape measure. A tailored wool bow, backed with the lining fabric, is sewn onto the front fold so the case resembles a miniature clutch bag to be kept on show in your sewing corner or dressing table. A pinboard is invaluable for fabric and ribbon swatches or just cuttings you find inspirational!

SEE PAGE 136 FOR INSTRUCTIONS

# Bow Belle Frames

VINTAGE MAGAZINES ARE TREASURE TROVES OF CHARISMATIC imagery, with the stylish illustrations, photography, and typography all encapsulating the essence of a particular era. Even the printing techniques used at this time enhance their unique quality—the illustrative images often feature broad strokes of intense color, held within elegant black linework. To showcase a page taken from an old magazine, just find an old frame, update it with a fresh coat of paint in a complementary color, and add a trio of enchanting silk bows, in differing shades, to highlight the images.

SEE PAGE 138 FOR INSTRUCTIONS

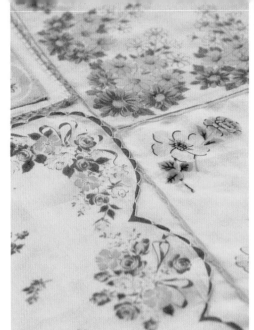
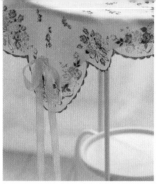

# Teatime Tablecloth

A LITTLE QUIRKY, BUT SO CUTE...! THIS TABLECLOTH is made from four handkerchiefs from the 1930s, printed in delightful floral patterns; some with pretty scalloped or picot edging. The fun is to choose ones that go well together to make a patchwork design. Just use as many as you need to cover your table, and if by any chance one is too small just layer it over another plainer one. Narrow old-fashioned rayon ribbons—a different color at each corner—are attached and tied in bows. Seeing the potential in a few vintage finds makes teatime extra sweet!

SEE PAGE 139 FOR INSTRUCTIONS

# Instructions

*On the following pages you will find*
*step-by-step instructions and diagrams for all the*
*projects featured.*

# Embellished Silk Cushions

## YOU WILL NEED

-------------------------------------

*48 in. (1.2 m) silk dupion*

*14-in. (35-cm) square
pillow form (cushion pad)*

*10-in. (26-cm) square lace
handkerchief*

*Mother-of-pearl button*

*Matching sewing thread*

*Needle, scissors, pins*

*Sewing machine*

-------------------------------------

**NOTE:** These instructions will
show you how to make the
emerald square cushion with
easy flange (see page 12). You
can also make the cushion
without the flange—simply
adjust your measurements
accordingly. A circular piece of
lace or crochet doily can be
used to adorn an existing
round cushion cover for an
easy alternative.

**1** For the front of this simple
flange pillow, cut a square of silk
dupion 21 x 21 in. (52 x 52 cm).
Position the lace handkerchief on the
right side of the fabric in the center of
the square. Pin and hand stitch in place with
tiny invisible stitches.

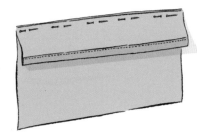

**2** For the back, cut two pieces of silk
dupion to 21 x 12 in. (52 x 30 cm)
and one piece that is 21 x 5 in.
(52 x 12 cm). Turn a ⅜-in. (1-cm)
hem to the wrong side along one
21-in. (52-cm) edge of the smaller piece and machine or hand stitch
in place. With right sides together, place the smaller piece over one
of the larger pieces so that the two long unhemmed edges line up,
and pin together.

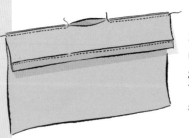

**3** Using a ¾-in. (2-cm) seam allowance,
machine stitch along the edge, but leave a
gap 1¼ in. (3 cm) at the center of the seam.
Turn so the right sides are facing outward
and press.

**4** For the loop, cut a strip of fabric 4¾ x
1½ in. (12 x 4 cm). Fold ½ in. (1 cm) to the
wrong side along both long edges and then fold in half
again so that you have a strip 4¾ x ½ in. (12 x 1 cm). Pin and
hand sew with tiny invisible stitches. Press.

**5** Fold the loop in half and slot into the open edge of the seam by ¾ in. (2 cm), so that 1½ in. (4 cm) of the loop is showing. Machine stitch the seam closed on the wrong side of the fabric.

**6** Finish the back by turning a ⅜-in. (1-cm) hem to the wrong side along one 21-in. (52-cm) edge of the other back piece and machine or hand stitch in place.

**7** To assemble the cover, place the piece with the loop over the front piece, right sides facing, so that the raw edges are level and the loop is in the center. Position the second back piece, right sides facing, over the top so that the hemmed edges overlap and the raw edges are level. Pin in place and then machine stitch around the outer edge, leaving a ¾-in. (2-cm) seam allowance. Trim the corners at the diagonal.

**8** Turn the cover right side out, push out all the corners, and press. For the flange, measure in from the outer edge by 3 in. (7 cm) all round and mark with pins. Stitch a line of basting (tacking) stitches along this line and then machine stitch. Sew a mother-of-pearl button to the back of the cover opposite to the loop.

# Silk *and* Lace Bolster

**1** Cut the silk fabric to 40 x 64 in. (1 x 1.6 m). Hand or machine stitch a ½-in. (1-cm) hem around all four sides and then press. Along one of the longer edges, turn back the silk fabric by 2 in. (5 cm), with right sides facing, and press flat. Machine stitch closely along the fold, about ⅛ in. (3 mm) in from the folded edge. Turn this fold back again, wrong sides facing, and press. This will be the end for the buttonholes.

## You will need
-------------------------------------------

*Lace panel (the piece we used measured 20 x 14 in./50 x 35 cm)*

*52 x 64 in. (1.3 x 1.6 m) silk fabric*

*20 x 6 in. (50 x 15 cm) bolster form*

*3 mother-of-pearl buttons*

*Matching sewing thread*

*Needle, scissors, pins*

*Tailor's chalk (optional)*

*Sewing machine*

**2** To mark out the positions for the lace and buttonholes, place the bolster form at the other long end, opposite to the buttonhole edge, and roll it up, making sure the bolster is in the center of the fabric or the cushion will be out of alignment. With a needle and thread or tailor's chalk, mark out the three buttonholes, ½ in. (1 cm) in from the folded edge and lined up horizontally to the edge. The middle buttonhole should be in the center with a buttonhole 4 in. (10 cm) along on each side. Make sure the buttonholes are to the correct length of each button. Lay the lace panel in position and pin in place.

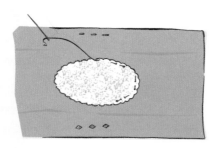

**3** Machine or hand stitch the buttonholes with matching thread. Hand stitch the lace carefully around the edge with tiny invisible stitches. Press. Roll up the bolster again and mark out where each button will go. Sew the buttons in place.

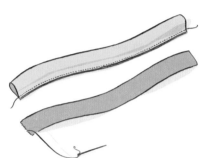

**4** For the ties, use the remaining silk fabric to cut two lengths of silk, each 64 x 6 in. (1.6 m x 15 cm). Fold each tie in half lengthwise, right sides facing, and machine along the long edge ½ in. (1 cm) from the edge and across one short edge. Turn right way out and press flat. Turn in the open end, pin, and hand stitch closed. Press.

**5** Roll up the bolster form in the fabric, fasten the buttons, and use the ties to secure each end with a bow. Alternatively, use a matching vintage ribbon.

# Silk Satin Pouches

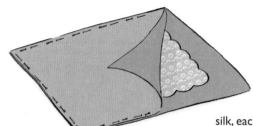

*Crochet or lace placemat, approximately 11 x 15 in. (28 x 38 cm)*

*24 x 24 in. (60 x 60 cm) piece of silk fabric*

*16-in. (40 cm) thin interlining*

*Matching sewing thread*

*Needle, scissors*

*Pins suitable for silk*

*Diamante brooch or mother-of-pearl buckle*

*Sewing machine*

1 Cut two pieces from the silk, each 12 x 16 in. (30 x 40 cm). The silk pieces should be ¾ in. (2 cm) longer and wider than your chosen crochet or lace piece so adjust these measurements if necessary. Hand stitch the crochet onto the right side of one piece of silk, centered in the middle. With right sides facing, pin and then baste (tack) the two pieces of silk together. Machine stitch down each long side and across one short side, leaving a ½-in. (1-cm) seam allowance. Trim corners at the diagonal. Lightly press the seams open. (When ironing silk, never use the steam setting or spray because water will mark the fabric.)

2 Turn inside out and lightly press again. Cut a piece of interlining 11 x 15 in. (28 x 38 cm). Alter these measurements if necessary to fit the size of your chosen crochet or lace piece. Slip the interlining into the pouch; if it is too snug, trim slightly until it fits.

3 Before closing the open edge, fold over twice to form the pouch, with the crochet or lace on the outside. Lightly press the two folds. The machined edge will be the outer flap, the open edge will be on the inner side. Turn in the open seam pulling in any excess silk caused naturally when the pouch is folded over. Pin and hand stitch closed with tiny invisible slipstitches.

**4** Pin along each side seam to form the pocket. Hand stitch the sides with tiny invisible slipstitches.

**5** For the pouch with the buckle and tie, cut a length of fabric 24 x 3 in. (60 x 7 cm). With right sides facing, fold in half lengthwise and pin. Machine or hand stitch, leaving a ½-in. (1-cm) seam allowance. Turn right side out and press. Tuck in each short end and hand stitch closed with tiny invisible stitches. Press. Thread the tie through the buckle, then stitch the buckle in place on the front flap of the pouch. For the diamanté brooch version, simply pin the brooch through the top layer of silk and the interlining.

# Frou-frou Lampshade

You will need
------------------------------------

*12 x 28 in. (30 x 70 cm)
silk dupion*

*Vintage lace panel
(we used a piece
12 x 44 in./30 x 110 cm)*

*12 in. (30 cm) of
1½-in (4-cm) wide
Petersham ribbon
to match*

*Wire lampshade frame,
4 in. (10 cm) in diameter
(top), 8 in. (20 cm) in
diameter (base), diagonal
height 6¾ in. (17 cm)*

*Matching sewing thread*

*Coordinating button or
buttons*

*Needle, scissors, pins*

*Sewing machine
(optional)*

------------------------------------

**SAFETY NOTE:** Always
use a low-wattage bulb.

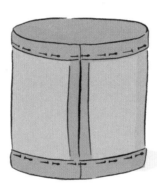

**1** To cover the lampshade frame, cut the silk to 12 x 28 in. (30 x 70 cm). With wrong sides facing, pin and baste (tack) the two shorter edges together. Machine stitch a seam ½ in. (1 cm) in from the edge. Press the seam open.

**2** Hem the top and bottom edges of the silk by turning ½ in. (1 cm) to the wrong side and then the same amount again. Pin and then stitch in place by hand or machine. Press and turn the fabric right side out.

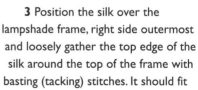

**3** Position the silk over the lampshade frame, right side outermost and loosely gather the top edge of the silk around the top of the frame with basting (tacking) stitches. It should fit neatly at the top of the shade with ¾ in. (2 cm) showing above the top of the rim and the rest hanging 2½ in. (6 cm) below the base.

**4** The lace panel shown in the photograph has a scalloped edge but any lace with a pretty edge can work. Position the lace over the silk and gather with large pleats until it fits around the silk with the scalloped edges meeting at the back. Pin in place and baste (tack) ¾ in. (2 cm) down from the top edge.

**5** To secure both layers, pin the Petersham ribbon in place around the top of the lace and silk so that the top ¾ in. (2 cm) is covered. Hand stitch the ribbon in place, overlapping the ribbon ends at the back.

**6** Flip the Petersham band over to the inside of the shade. Sew your chosen button or buttons at the top of the scalloped lace edging.

# Filigree Curtain

1 Measure the required finished size of the curtain and add on 8 in. (20 cm) to the width for fullness and hems, and 6 in. (15 cm) to the length. Cut the fabric to this size. Press ⅜ in. (1 cm) double hems to the wrong side along both side edges and machine stitch in place. Press a double 1½-in (4-cm) hem across the lower edge and machine stitch in place. To make a casing for the curtain rod, press 3 in. (8 cm) to the wrong side along the top edge, pin, and then machine stitch in place. Add another line of stitching, this time 1 in. (2.5 cm) from the top edge. Slip the curtain rod through the casing and fix in place.

*Sheer cotton voile or net fabric*

*Curtain rod*

*Selection of doilies*

*Matching sewing thread*

*Needles, scissors, pins*

*Sewing machine*

2 Gather together as many doilies as necessary to cover the size of your curtain. Choose a selection with differing intricate patterns, both machine-made and handmade. With the curtain still hanging, position the doilies randomly and pin in place, repositioning any as you go.

3 Take the curtain down and hand stitch each doily onto the curtain using small neat stitches. Press the curtain and then re-hang.

# Lace *and* Burmese Cotton Runner

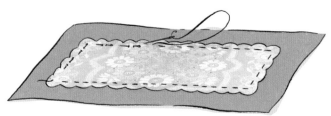

1 Position the lace panel on top of the cotton, so that it is evenly spaced all round. Pin, baste (tack) and then hand stitch the lace in place. Burmese cotton comes in narrow widths of 24 in. (60 cm) so if you are using another cotton you will need to cut and hem the piece to a width of 24 in. (60 cm).

2 Fray each short end of the runner by gently pulling the threads away from the fabric edge until you have a fringe that is approximately ¼ in. (5 mm) deep. For a more durable fringe, add a line of machine stitching ¼ in. (5 mm) from the edge before fraying. If using linen fabric, simply hem the edges instead of fraying.

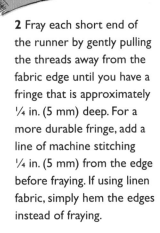

### YOU WILL NEED

--------------------------------------

*Vintage lace panel, approximately 40 x 15 in. (100 x 38 cm)*

*60 x 24 in. (150 x 60 cm) piece of Burmese cotton (see Note)*

*Matching sewing thread*

*Needle, scissors, pins*

*Sewing machine (optional)*

--------------------------------------

**NOTE**: Burmese cotton is very similar to burlap (hessian) in appearance but is much softer. It comes in narrow 24-in. (60-cm) widths so is perfect for a table runner. Use a fine linen fabric if you prefer.

# Doily Corsage Napkins

**1** Cut the Burmese cotton into four napkins, each measuring 12 x 12 in. (30 x 30 cm). Fray the edges by gently pulling the threads away from the fabric edge, until you have a "fringe" all around that is approximately ¼ in. (5 mm) deep. For a more durable fringe, add a line of machine stitching ¼ in. (5 mm) from the edge before fraying. If using linen fabric, simply hem the edges instead of fraying.

## You will need

-----------------------------------------

*24-in. (60-cm) square of Burmese cotton or linen fabric (see Note)*

*Floristry wire or light garden wire*

*Four vintage doilies*

*Matching sewing thread*

*Needle, scissors*

*Tissue paper*

*Spray adhesive*

*Four lengths of ½-in. (1-cm) wide ribbon*

*Sewing machine (optional)*

-----------------------------------------

**NOTE**: Burmese cotton has a texture similar to burlap (hessian) but is much softer. Use a fine linen fabric as an alternative.

**2** For the flower stems, cut four lengths of wire each measuring 4 in. (10 cm). Fold each doily in half, then in half again, and slip over the top ½ in. (1 cm) of wire. Twist each doily at the base to form a pleasing flower shape and then, with needle and thread, sew around the base so that each flower holds its shape and fits tightly against the wire.

**3** Use scissors to cut several ½-in. (1-cm) strips of tissue paper. Apply a light coating of spray adhesive to one side and then wrap the tissue strips around each wire to cover the stems and the base of the doily flower. When the tissue is almost dry, smooth out the surface by lightly pressing the tissue.

**4** To assemble your napkins, loosely roll each napkin and tie with a piece of ribbon. Tuck the doily corsage inside the ribbon.

# Tissue *and* Lace Gift Bags

**1** For the front of the bag, cut out a double layer of tissue paper 12 x 10 in. (30 x 25 cm). Use as many layers of tissue as necessary for a stronger color. The bags in these photographs have two layers, making them slightly translucent. Cut out a piece of lace 12 x 10 in. (30 x 25 cm), with the scalloped edge at one of the shorter ends. If you don't have lace with a scalloped edge, then any pretty edge will do. Lay the lace over the tissue layers, right side up, with the scalloped edge at the top. Pin and baste (tack) the lace to the tissue. Repeat this step to create the back of the bag.

YOU WILL NEED

----------------------------------------

*Tissue paper*

*20 x 20 in. (50 x 50 cm) square of lace, scalloped edges optional*

*Matching sewing thread*

*Needle, scissors, pins*

*Sewing machine*

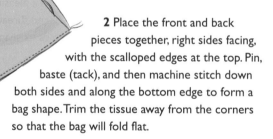

**2** Place the front and back pieces together, right sides facing, with the scalloped edges at the top. Pin, baste (tack), and then machine stitch down both sides and along the bottom edge to form a bag shape. Trim the tissue away from the corners so that the bag will fold flat.

**3** Turn the bag right way out so that the lace is on the outside, pushing out the corners. Carefully trim away the overlapping tissue at the top of the bag, and with needle and matching sewing thread sew the tissue to the lace around the top with tiny running stitches, $\frac{1}{16}$ in. (1 mm) in from the edge.

# Lace Jewelry Roll

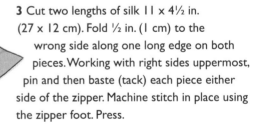

**1** For the inside of the jewelry roll, cut a piece of silk 21 x 11 in. (52 x 27 cm). Use this as the base on which to layer each section. The finished roll will measure 20 x 10 in. (50 x 25 cm). Cut another piece of silk 11 x 4½ in. (27 x 12 cm) and a piece of lining fabric 11 x 7 in. (27 x 17 cm): this will be the pocket. With right sides facing, pin and machine these two pieces together along one long side, taking a ½-in. (1-cm) seam allowance. Press the seam open. Fold the long raw edge of the silk over by ½ in. (1 cm) and press. With the inside of the jewelry roll facing right side up, position the pocket so that the stitched seam is 8½ in. (21 cm) from the left-hand side. Pin and baste (tack) the cotton lining in place, leaving the silk flap free.

## YOU WILL NEED

--------------------------------------------

*24 x 24 in. (60 x 60 cm) gray silk dupion*

*21 x 11 in. (52 x 27 cm) piece of lace*

*12 in. (30 cm) cotton lining fabric*

*7 in. (18 cm) white zipper*

*16 in. (40 cm) narrow velvet ribbon*

*Two glass buttons*

*Diamanté brooch*

*Matching sewing thread*

*Needle, scissors, pins*

*Sewing machine*

**2** For the zippered pocket section, cut two pieces of silk each 2½ x 1¼ in. (6 x 3 cm). Fold ½ in. (1 cm) to the wrong side of one short edge and machine this over each end of the zipper, right sides up and stitching close to the fold. Stitch the other piece of fabric to the other end of the zipper in the same way.

**3** Cut two lengths of silk 11 x 4½ in. (27 x 12 cm). Fold ½ in. (1 cm) to the wrong side along one long edge on both pieces. Working with right sides uppermost, pin and then baste (tack) each piece either side of the zipper. Machine stitch in place using the zipper foot. Press.

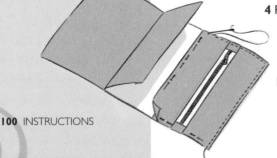

**4** Position the zippered pocket right side up, so that the right-hand edge lines up with the right-hand side of the jewelry roll main piece and the left-hand edge overlaps the cotton lining. Pin and baste (tack) in place, leaving the silk flap loose.

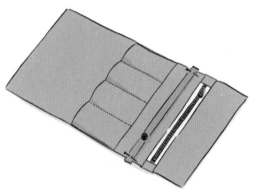

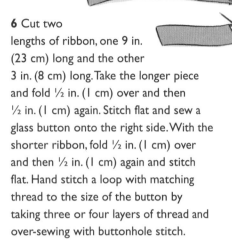

**5** Flip down the silk flap and baste (tack) in place. Machine stitch closely along the folded edge, then machine stitch three lines to make four pockets. Space each line evenly apart, allowing for the ½ in (1 cm) seam allowance, so that each pocket measures approximately 2½ in. (6.25 cm) wide. Machine stitch a line down the left-hand side of the zipper, ½ in. (1 cm) from the edge of the fabric.

**6** Cut two lengths of ribbon, one 9 in. (23 cm) long and the other 3 in. (8 cm) long. Take the longer piece and fold ½ in. (1 cm) over and then ½ in. (1 cm) again. Stitch flat and sew a glass button onto the right side. With the shorter ribbon, fold ½ in. (1 cm) over and then ½ in. (1 cm) again and stitch flat. Hand stitch a loop with matching thread to the size of the button by taking three or four layers of thread and over-sewing with buttonhole stitch.

**7** Pin the ribbons in position between the zipper and the four-pocket section, so that the loop and button match up.

**8** For the outer layer of the jewelry roll, cut another piece of silk 21 x 11 in. (52 x 27 cm) and hand stitch the lace panel to the right side of the silk. Pin and baste (tack) the inner and outer layers together, right sides facing, and machine stitch around all four sides with a ½-in. (1-cm) seam allowance, leaving an opening 5 in. (12 cm) at the short end farthest from the zippered pocket. Trim the corners at the diagonal. Turn the jewelry roll right way out through this opening and push out all four corners. Press flat. Hand stitch a loop to the size of the other glass button following step 6, at the center point of the seam. Hand stitch to close up the seam. Fold the jewelry roll over and mark the position of the glass button so that it matches up with the loop. Stitch in place. For decoration, pin a brooch to the outside near the loop.

# Lace and Ribbon Tie-backs

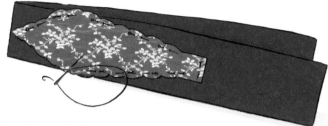

YOU WILL NEED

--------------------------------------------

*60 in. (150 cm) ribbon,
approximately
4 in. (10 cm) wide*

*Piece of antique lace,
approximately
18 in. (45 cm) long*

*Vintage clasp or buckle*

*Two curtain rings, about
1½ in. (4 cm) in diameter*

*Matching sewing thread*

*Needle, scissors, pins*

**1** Fold the ribbon in half, wrong sides together, so that the right side of the ribbon is facing you. Pin the lace piece to the front of the ribbon, close to the fold, so that it faces you when the curtain is held in place. Slipstitch the lace to the ribbon, using tiny invisible stitches.

**2** Thread the clasp or buckle on to the ribbon so that it sits near the lace. Work out where to position the two curtain rings, depending on how full your curtain fabric is. Attach a curtain ring to the wrong side of each ribbon end with a few stitches and then thread the end of the ribbon through each one. These rings will be placed over a curtain hook fastened to the wall to hold the curtain in place. Cut the ends of the ribbon in a diagonal to finish.

# Handkerchief Café Curtain

**1** Place the selection of handkerchiefs on a flat surface and arrange, right sides up, as required to fit your window. They won't be all an identical size so just adjust to make a pleasing arrangement. Pin the edges together, in this position, and then stitch together by hand, catching the corners together, and then stitching only at intermittent intervals along the edges. At this stage, hold the curtain up to the window to see if more stitches are needed, but some gaps between the handkerchiefs add to the appeal.

YOU WILL NEED

-------------------------------------------

*Nine handkerchiefs
(ours were approximately
10½ in./26 cm square)*

*4½ yds (4 m) white rayon
ribbon, 1½ in. (4 cm) wide*

*Matching sewing thread*

*Needle, scissors, pins*

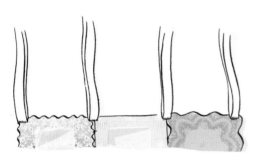

**2** Cut four 1-yd (1-m) lengths of ribbon, fold each one in half, and hand stitch each ribbon along the fold to the top of the curtain and on the wrong side—there should be one each end and two in the center where the handkerchiefs are joined. Loop over your curtain rail and tie in loose bows. Trim the ends of the ribbons diagonally.

# Handkerchief Envelopes

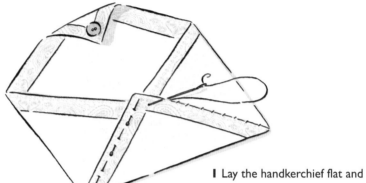

*Vintage handkerchief*

*Spray starch*

*Vintage button*

*Matching sewing thread*

*Needle, scissors, pins*

*Sheet of 140-lb (300-gsm) watercolor paper*

*Magazine*

*Scalpel and cutting board*

*Safety ruler*

*Double-sided sticky tape or adhesive suitable for paper*

*Ribbon (optional)*

**1** Lay the handkerchief flat and press using spray starch to give crispness. Fold the corners in to create an envelope shape, pin, then hand stitch the bottom flap to the two side flaps with invisible slipstitches. Press. Sew a button to the point of the upper flap on the right side.

**2** Cut the watercolor paper to a size that fits the envelope easily, either folded into a card or alternatively as a single postcard. Cut letters from the magazine, using a scalpel and ruler, to spell a message or name. Glue these to the card using adhesive or double-sided sticky tape. For decoration add a loop of ribbon to your card if you wish.

# Nostalgia Notebook

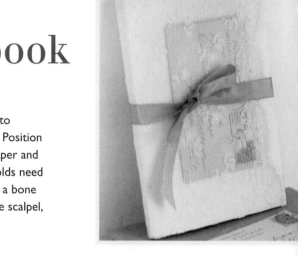

**1** Cut the watercolor paper to 8¾ x 12¾ in. (22 x 32 cm). Position the notebook over the paper and mark where the spine folds need to be. Score them with a bone folder or the blunt side of the scalpel, and then fold.

**2** Cut the tulle to 10 x 14 in. (25 x 35 cm) and cut the lace so that the scalloped edge is 10 in. (25 cm) long. Lay the tulle over the outside of the watercolor paper and position the lace on top, so that the scalloped edge will eventually line up with the edge of the front cover. It can even overlap the edge slightly. If the lace trim is smaller than the tulle and has a frayed edge, stitch a tiny hem to neaten. Hand stitch the lace to the tulle along the plain or hemmed edge with tiny stitches, leaving the pretty edge open. Tack the lace to the tulle along the top and bottom to make it easier handle when glueing in place. Press.

**3** Add a strip of double-sided sticky tape along each edge of the watercolor paper on the inside. Lay the tulle and lace over the outside of the watercolor paper, so the pretty edge lines up with the front cover edge, and fold over the fabric to adhere to the sticky tape, pulling gently to avoid any air pockets. A tiny piece of extra tape might be needed on the inside to secure the folded corners of the tulle. Make sure the pretty edge of the lace along the front edge isn't glued down.

**4** Add a strip of double-sided tape all around the outside edge of the notebook and down the spine. Carefully position the notebook inside the lace and paper cover and press firmly to adhere. Place under a heavy book to press flat. When you are finished, slip a vintage postcard between the lace and tulle on the front cover.

## You will need

-------------------------------------------

Sheet of 140-lb (300-gsm) watercolor paper

Notebook, 8½ x 6 x ½ in. (21 x 15 x 1 cm) in size

Piece of tulle or fine net, at least 10 x 14 in. (25 x 35 cm)

Piece of vintage lace with scalloped edge

Vintage postcard

Pencil

Ruler

Scalpel and cutting board

Double-sided tape

Bone folder (optional)

Matching sewing thread to match

Needle, scissors

# Rose Card

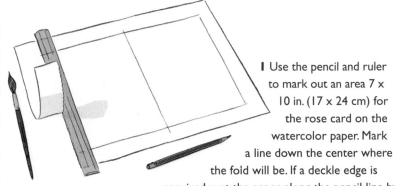

**1** Use the pencil and ruler to mark out an area 7 x 10 in. (17 x 24 cm) for the rose card on the watercolor paper. Mark a line down the center where the fold will be. If a deckle edge is required, wet the paper along the pencil line by dipping a paintbrush into water and wiping along the line to dampen. When the paper is soft hold a ruler firmly against the line and tear the paper against the ruler's edge. Alternatively, for a clean edge cut out the card with ruler and scalpel.

## You will need

Sheet of 140-lb (300-gsm) watercolor paper

16 in. (40 cm) grosgrain ribbon, ½ in. (1 cm) wide

Pencil

Safety ruler

Scalpel and cutting board

Bone folder (optional)

Eraser

Tracing paper

Rose template (see page 140)

Acrylic paint

Sable paintbrush

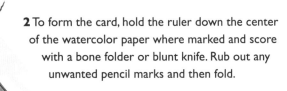

**2** To form the card, hold the ruler down the center of the watercolor paper where marked and score with a bone folder or blunt knife. Rub out any unwanted pencil marks and then fold.

**3** Using a sheet of tracing paper and a pencil, trace over the rose template (see page 140). Turn the tracing paper over and rub the back with the pencil to cover the template image. Turn over and position the tracing paper over the watercolor paper so the image is on the front of the card. Follow the outline of the image with a sharp pencil, pressing firmly so that the rose appears lightly on the card.

**4** Mix acrylic paint with water to the desired consistency (you can use watercolor paint or colored pencils if you prefer) and paint the rose.

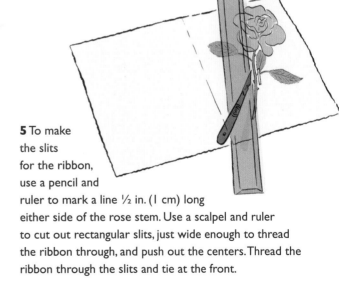

**5** To make the slits for the ribbon, use a pencil and ruler to mark a line ½ in. (1 cm) long either side of the rose stem. Use a scalpel and ruler to cut out rectangular slits, just wide enough to thread the ribbon through, and push out the centers. Thread the ribbon through the slits and tie at the front.

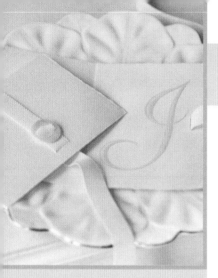

# Concertina Card

**1** Use a pencil and ruler to mark out three cards, each 5½ x 3½ in. (14 x 9 cm), on the watercolor paper. If a deckle edge is required, see step 1 of Rose Card on page 106. Alternatively, for a clean edge, use a scalpel and safety ruler to cut out the cards. Transfer and paint your chosen letter, from a book or old magazine, on to one of the cards (see steps 3 and 4 of Rose Card on page 107.)

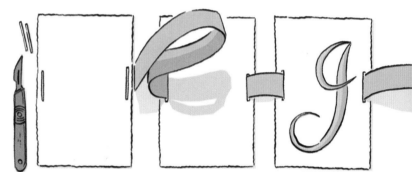

**2** To make the slits for the ribbon, use a pencil and ruler to mark a vertical line ¾ in. (2 cm) long, approximately ½ in. (1 cm) in from the left and right side of each card and 2½ in. (6 cm) down from the top. Use a scalpel and ruler to cut out rectangular slits, just wide enough to thread the ribbon through, and push out the centers. Rub out any remaining pencil marks. Thread the ribbon through all the slits to create a concertina effect. Slot the buckle on to the ribbon at the end.

## YOU WILL NEED

-------------------------------------------

*Sheet of 140-lb (300-gsm) watercolor paper*

*36 in. (90 cm) grosgrain ribbon ¾ in. (2 cm) wide*

*Mother-of-pearl buckle (to fit ribbon)*

*Tracing paper*

*Pencil*

*Safety ruler*

*Scalpel and cutting board*

*Acrylic paint*

*Sable paintbrush*

*Eraser*

# Slotted Ribbon Box

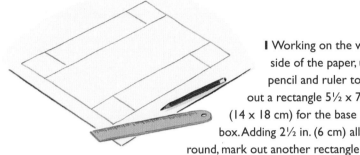

**1** Working on the wrong side of the paper, use a pencil and ruler to mark out a rectangle 5½ x 7 in. (14 x 18 cm) for the base of the box. Adding 2½ in. (6 cm) all round, mark out another rectangle 10 x 12 in. (26 x 30 cm). Use a bone folder or blunt knife to score the inner rectangle, following the pencil lines. Between the inner and outer pencil marks, using a ruler and scalpel, cut away each 2½ in. (6 cm) corner.

YOU WILL NEED

----------------------------------------

*Sheet of 140-lb (300-gsm) watercolor paper*

*60 in. (150 cm) of 1-in. (2.5-cm) wide grosgrain ribbon*

*Pencil*

*Safety ruler*

*Bone folder (optional)*

*Scalpel and cutting board*

*Eraser*

*Glassine paper (optional)*

**2** Before folding up the sides, use a pencil and ruler to mark out the slits 1 in. (2.5 cm) deep for the ribbon, ½ in. (1 cm) along from each corner and then again, another ½ in. (1 cm) along from that. Using a scalpel and ruler, cut out each slit, so that the ribbon will thread snugly through without being too loose. When you have cut all the slits, erase any pencil marks.

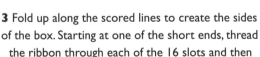

**3** Fold up along the scored lines to create the sides of the box. Starting at one of the short ends, thread the ribbon through each of the 16 slots and then loop at the front. For the optional paper lining, cut out the glassine to the size of the box, adding an extra 4 in. (10 cm) all around to fold over the gift.

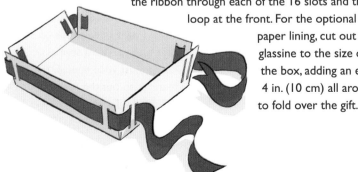

# Beribboned Tags

**1** Use the pencil and ruler to mark out each tag to a measurement of 4 x 3 in. (10 x 7 cm) on the watercolor paper. To create a deckle edge, wet the paper along the pencil line by dipping a paintbrush into water and wiping along the line to dampen. When the paper is soft, hold a ruler firmly against the line and tear the paper against the ruler's edge.

YOU WILL NEED

-------------------------------------------

Sheet of 140-lb (300-gsm) watercolor paper

20 in. (50 cm) grosgrain ribbon ½ in. (1 cm) wide

Pencil

Safety ruler

Scalpel and cutting board

Tracing paper

Rosebud and daisy templates on pages 140 and 141

Acrylic paint

Sable paintbrush

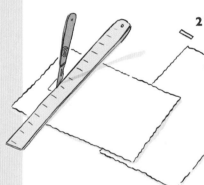

**2** Wait until the paper is dry. For the slit at the top of the tag, use the pencil and ruler to mark a ½ in. (1 cm) long line, ¼ in. (5 mm) down from the top edge and 1¼ in. (3 cm) in from each side. Cut a very narrow slit with a scalpel and ruler, and push out the center. This should fit your ribbon.

**3** For the decorative image, place tracing paper over the rosebud or daisy template (pages 140 and 141) or a letter or number copied from a book or old magazine, and trace the outline in pencil. Turn the tracing paper over and rub the back with pencil to cover the template image. Turn the tracing paper back again and position over the tag. Follow the outline with a sharp pencil, pressing firmly so that the image appears lightly on the tag.

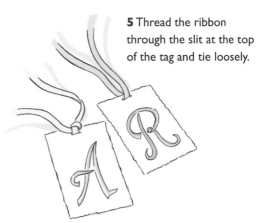

**5** Thread the ribbon through the slit at the top of the tag and tie loosely.

**4** Mix acrylic paint with water to the desired consistency (use watercolor paint or colored pencils if you prefer,) and paint the image.

# Vintage Scarf
# Chairbacks

**1** Cut two panels from the linen fabric, one 8¾ x 14 in. (22 x 35 cm) and another 16½ x 14 in. (41 x 35 cm)—this allows for seam allowances of ⅝ in. (1.5 cm). Cut a backing panel, also from linen, that is 33 x 14 in. (82 x 35 cm). From the silk scarf cut a panel that is 8¾ x 14 in. (22 x 35 cm), making sure you choose an area of the scarf that shows the pattern at its best.

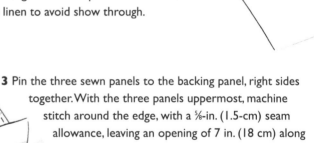

**2** With right sides together, pin the smaller linen panel to the silk scarf panel, along the long edge. Machine stitch with a ⅝-in. (1.5-cm) seam allowance. Repeat to join the other piece of linen to the other edge of the silk panel. Press the seams toward the linen to avoid show through.

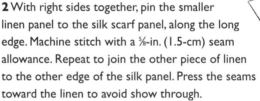

**3** Pin the three sewn panels to the backing panel, right sides together. With the three panels uppermost, machine stitch around the edge, with a ⅝-in. (1.5-cm) seam allowance, leaving an opening of 7 in. (18 cm) along the short edge of the bottom panel (this will fall to the back of the chair.) Trim the corners to remove excess bulk.

**4** Turn right way out, pushing out all the corners and press. Turn the seams at the open end under and hand stitch closed with tiny slipstitches. Cut two lengths of ribbon, each 40 in. (1 m), and turn a tiny hem over at one end of each length. Hand stitch to each side of the back panel, halfway down the silk scarf panel. You may need to adjust the ribbon position depending on the measurements of your chair.

# Jeweled Mirror

**1** Take your mirror to a glazier and have it cut into four equal pieces. Ask for the edges to be slightly ground so they are safe to handle. Arrange the pieces with the back (coated) sides uppermost. Cut strips of double-sided tape to match the thickness of your mirror and stick to the four inner cut edges as shown in the diagram—you only need to apply tape to the top left and bottom right inner edges. Press together firmly so all four mirrors are aligned.

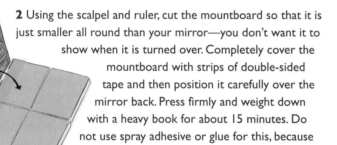

**2** Using the scalpel and ruler, cut the mountboard so that it is just smaller all round than your mirror—you don't want it to show when it is turned over. Completely cover the mountboard with strips of double-sided tape and then position it carefully over the mirror back. Press firmly and weight down with a heavy book for about 15 minutes. Do not use spray adhesive or glue for this, because it may eat into the mirror backing.

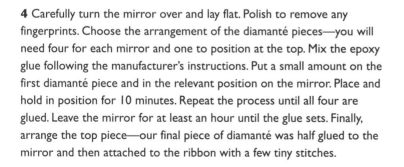

**3** Fold the ribbon in half to form a loop. Pinch both ends into a pleat, place a strip of double-sided tape to join together, and then, with another strip of double-sided tape, attach to the top center of the mountboard so that a loop of approximately 5½ in. (14 cm) shows above the mirror. Cut a piece of felt to the same size as the mountboard. Spray the felt with adhesive and attach to the mountboard. Press the felt down firmly.

**4** Carefully turn the mirror over and lay flat. Polish to remove any fingerprints. Choose the arrangement of the diamanté pieces—you will need four for each mirror and one to position at the top. Mix the epoxy glue following the manufacturer's instructions. Put a small amount on the first diamanté piece and in the relevant position on the mirror. Place and hold in position for 10 minutes. Repeat the process until all four are glued. Leave the mirror for at least an hour until the glue sets. Finally, arrange the top piece—our final piece of diamanté was half glued to the mirror and then attached to the ribbon with a few tiny stitches.

## YOU WILL NEED

*Piece of mirror, ¼ in. (5 mm) thick and approximately 9¼ x 7½ in. (23 x 19 cm) in size*

*14 in. (35 cm) metallic ribbon, 2½ in. (6 cm) wide*

*High-tack double-sided craft tape*

*Piece of heavyweight mountboard*

*Safety ruler*

*Scalpel and cutting board*

*Piece of felt*

*Spray adhesive suitable for fabric*

*Five pieces of diamanté jewelry*

*Super strong epoxy resin glue, suitable for metal and glass*

*Needle and matching sewing thread (optional)*

**NOTE:** Make a single mirror in the same way but omit the mountboard.

**SAFETY NOTE:** This mirror cannot be hung. Just prop in a safe position and keep out of reach of small children. Be sure to ask your glazier to smooth the edges of the mirror after cutting it for you, because they can be sharp.

# Vintage Drawstring Bags

**1** Cut the linen to 32 x 10½ in. (80 x 26 cm) and fold in half to create a bag that is 15½ x 9½ in. (39 x 24 cm). The right side of the fabric should be on the outside and the folded edge at the bottom. For the pocket, cut the patterned fabric to approximately 5½ x 6½ in. (14 x 16 cm). Alter these measurements to suit the size of the decorative image you want to show. Turn in the top edge of the pocket by ½ in. (1 cm), then by ½ in. (1 cm) again, and machine stitch along this edge, ¼ in. (5 mm) from the edge. Turn ¼ in. (5 mm) to the wrong side along the side and bottom edges and press. Position the pocket on the front of the fabric and pin and baste (tack) in place. Machine stitch down the sides and along the bottom of the pocket, close to the edge, and press again.

## YOU WILL NEED (FOR EACH BAG)

----------------------------------------

*1 yd (1 m) linen fabric*

*16 in. (40 cm) vintage patterned cotton fabric*

*Matching sewing thread*

*Needle, scissors, pins*

*Sewing machine*

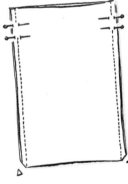

**2** Reverse the fabric so the wrong side is on the outside, fold into the bag shape again, and pin down each long side. To mark out the channel through which the ribbon ties are threaded, use pins to mark a point 2 in. (5 cm) down from the top edge and then 1¼ in. (3 cm) below this, on each side of the bag. Machine stitch down the sides of the bag, leaving a ½-in. (1-cm) seam allowance, except between the two marks made for the channel. Reverse stitch several times at the edge of each line so that when the ties are threaded through, the seams won't unravel. Trim the corners at the bottom and press open the seams.

----------------------------------------

*As an alternative, use seersucker fabric instead.*

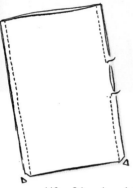

**3** For the bag lining, cut another piece of linen that is 32 x 10½ in. (80 x 26 cm). With right sides together, fold the fabric to 16 x 10½ in. (40 x 26 cm) and then pin and baste (tack) down both long edges, leaving a 6-in. (15-cm) gap open halfway down one side. Machine stitch, leaving a ½-in. (1-cm) seam allowance. Trim the corners at the bottom and press open the seams. Reverse the lining so the right side of the fabric is on the outside.

**4** Insert the lining into the outer bag so that the right sides of each are together. Line up the seams, then pin, baste (tack,) and machine stitch around the top, ½ in. (1 cm) down from the top edge.

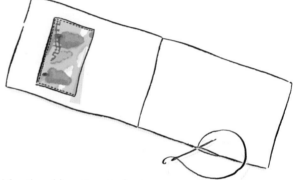

**5** Pull the outer bag through the open gap in the lining, and press. Hand stitch the opening closed using slipstitches. Now push the inner lining back inside the bag, push out all the corners, and press.

**6** To make the channel for the ribbon ties, pin, baste (tack) and machine stitch a line 1½ in. (4 cm) down from the top, all the way around the bag, and another 1¼ in. (3 cm) below this. This should be lined up with the top and bottom of the opening in the side seams.

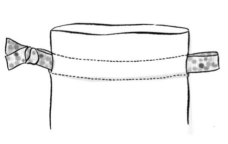

**7** For the handmade ribbon tie, cut a length of patterned fabric 36 x 3 in. (90 x 8 cm). Fold ½ in. (1 cm) to the wrong side along each long edge and then fold in half again lengthwise; press. Turn in each short end by ½ in. (1 cm) and then hand or machine stitch the seam closed; press. Thread the tie through the channel in the bag so you have a loop at one end and the tie ends are knotted at the other end.

# Blossom *and* Fern
# Tie Cushion

**1** Cut three pieces from the linen fabric, one 18 x 18 in. (45 x 45 cm), one 14 x 18 in. (35 x 45 cm), and another 11½ x 18 in. (29 x 45 cm). Take the smallest piece and machine stitch a line of zigzag stitch along one of the long edges, approximately ½ in. (1 cm) from the edge. This is to prevent fraying.

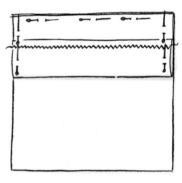

**2** Take this smaller piece and turn the stitched edge 4 in. (10 cm) to the wrong side. Pin and press. With right sides together, position this piece to the top of the 18 x 18 in. (45 x 45 cm) piece of linen, making sure the raw edges are lined up. Pin and baste (tack) together, leaving a ⅝-in. (1.5-cm) seam allowance along the top and sides.

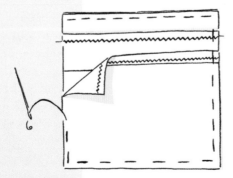

**3** Take the 14 x 18 in. (35 x 45 cm) piece of linen and turn ⅝ in. (1.5 cm) to the wrong side and machine stitch using zigzag stitch. Position this piece at the bottom of the 18 x 18 in. (45 x 45 cm) piece, right sides together. Pin and baste (tack) together, leaving a ⅝-in. (1.5-cm) seam allowance along the bottom and sides. At this stage gently insert your pad, and adjust the seam allowance if necessary.

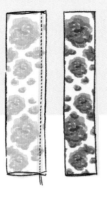

**4** For the ties cut two pieces from the scarf, one approximately 22¾ x 9½ in. (57 x 24 cm) and another 17¼ x 9½ in. (43 x 24 cm). Try to use the scarf's rolled edge, if possible. With right sides together, fold each piece in half, pin, and machine stitch down each long edge, leaving a seam allowance of 1 in. (2.5 cm). Turn the ties the right way out and press.

**5** Turn the cushion cover the right way out. Make a gap of 4 in. (10 cm) in the top seam by carefully opening up the basting (tacking) stitches. Insert ⅝ in. (1.5 cm) of the longer tie into the seam and pin in place. Repeat along the bottom seam with the shorter tie.

**6** Turn the cushion cover inside out again and machine stitch along the four seams. If you want to reduce fraying, machine stitch another line nearer to the raw edge. Remove the tacking stitches and trim each corner diagonally to reduce any bulk. Turn right side out and press.

**7** To add a patch to the front, cut a square from a leftover piece of the scarf, turn over ¼ in. (5 mm), and then another ¼ in. (5 mm), and press. Stitch to the front of the cushion with invisible slipstitches.

# Velvet Ribbon Throw

**1** Lay the wool fabric on a flat surface and gently roll a hem of about ⅝ in. (1.5 cm) to the wrong side. Pin and then hand stitch in place using invisible slipstitches.

## You will need

--------------------------------------------

*60 in. (1.5 m) wool fabric, approximately 58 in. (1.45 m) wide*

*136 in. (3.4 m) velvet ribbon, 1½ in. (4 cm) wide*

*Organza and silk corsage flower*

*Matching sewing thread*

*Pins suitable for wool and silk*

*Needle, scissors*

**2** Cut a length of ribbon to the width of the fabric, plus an extra 1¼ in. (3 cm). With the right side of the fabric facing up, pin the ribbon along both sides, approximately 10¼ in. (26 cm) from each selvedge, tucking ⅝ in. (1.5 cm) of ribbon neatly under at each end. Hand stitch both edges of the ribbon in place with invisible slipstitches. Hand stitch the folded ends of the ribbon to the fabric.

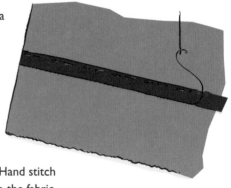

**3** Take the remaining length of ribbon, fold in half and pin the flower to this point, making sure the right sides of the velvet are uppermost. Then pin this in position onto the fabric wherever you wish. Finish by cutting the ends of the ribbon diagonally.

# Rosette Frame

**1** Find a frame that suits the size of your image. If necessary, remove old paint or varnish and repaint it. Using the scalpel, ruler, and cutting board, cut the polyboard to fit neatly within the back of the frame. Cut out the watercolor paper to the same size. Maybe choose a colored watercolor paper to match your image.

**2** Pick a beautiful fashion page from an old vintage magazine, that will fit comfortably within the size of your frame. Glue the back of the image with spray adhesive and position on the watercolor paper. Spray adhesive glue is ideal if used lightly—the image will not be damaged and can be peeled off if necessary. Assemble the paper, backed by the polyboard, into the picture frame and, using a picture framing kit, follow the maker's instructions to secure.

YOU WILL NEED

--------------------------------------

*Vintage picture frame*

*Vintage magazine image*

*1 yd (1 m) ribbon ½–¾ in. (1–2 cm) wide, in four or five colors*

*Sheet of polyboard*

*Sheet of 140-lb (300-gsm) watercolor paper*

*1½ x 1½ in. (4 x 4 cm) thin card*

*Spray adhesive*

*Picture framing kit (optional)*

*Scalpel and cutting board*

*Ruler*

*Needle, scissors*

*Matching sewing thread*

*Multipurpose glue suitable for wood and silk*

**3** Cut a circle of thin card 1½ in. (4 cm) in diameter. Choose a selection of four or five ribbons to match your chosen picture. Take a length of ribbon and fold over to make three loops. Secure the ribbon to the circle of card with a few stitches, at the central point where the loops overlap. Do the same with the next ribbon, positioning over the first loops so that they start to form a rosette. Stitch again. Continue until you have a pleasing array of loops, flaring out evenly from the center. With the final loop, hide the stitches by flipping the last ribbons over the top. Add multipurpose glue to the back of the rosette card and glue it to the picture frame.

# A La Mode Cards

**1** Mark out an area 7¼ x 9½ in. (18 x 24 cm) with the pencil and ruler on the watercolor paper and cut out using a scalpel and ruler. Mark a line down the center where the fold will be and score a line with a bone folder or blunt knife. Rub out the pencil marks and fold to form a card. Glue your image to the front of the card using spray adhesive. Position the image centered on the width but leaving a 1¼-in. (3-cm) margin at the top.

You will need (for one card)

------------------------------------

*Sheet of 140-lb (300-gsm) ivory watercolor paper*

*Photocopied illustration, 3½ x 2½ in. (9 x 6 cm)*

*1 yd (1 m) satin ribbon, approximately ¼–½ in. (5–10 mm) wide*

*Vintage diamanté brooch*

*Woven clothing label*

*Sheet of tracing or glassine paper*

*Pencil*

*Safety ruler*

*Scalpel and cutting board*

*Bone folder (optional)*

*Eraser*

*Spray adhesive*

*Double-sided tape or fabric and paper adhesive*

*Scissors*

*Newspaper*

**2** Center the label underneath the image, leaving a 1-in. (2.5-cm) gap between the image and the label. Turn the label edges under and glue these into position using double-sided tape or fabric adhesive.

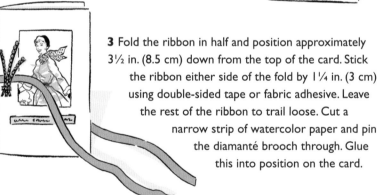

**3** Fold the ribbon in half and position approximately 3½ in. (8.5 cm) down from the top of the card. Stick the ribbon either side of the fold by 1¼ in. (3 cm) using double-sided tape or fabric adhesive. Leave the rest of the ribbon to trail loose. Cut a narrow strip of watercolor paper and pin the diamanté brooch through. Glue this into position on the card.

**4** Apply spray adhesive to a strip about ½ in. (1 cm) wide at the center crease (use newspaper to mask off the area.) Position the tracing paper inside the card. "Close" the card by tying the ribbon loosely.

# Diamanté Pendants

**1** With pencil and ruler, mark out a rectangle 6½ x 1¼ in. (16 x 3 cm) on the paper and cut out using a scalpel and safety ruler. Repeat to make as many pendants as you want. Punch a hole at the top of each pendant, about ½ in. (1 cm) from the top.

**2** Arrange anything from one to three items on the paper and glue them into position, using double epoxy glue (follow the manufacturer's instructions.) If you have a strand of diamanté, cut it to the width of the paper and glue into position at the bottom. Thread a length of ribbon through each hole.

**YOU WILL NEED**

------------------------------------------

*140-lb (300-gsm) watercolor or sheet of drawing (cartridge) paper*

*Various small pieces of diamanté*

*Glass buttons*

*Diamanté strand (optional)*

*1 yd (1 m) narrow satin ribbon for each pendant*

*Pencil*

*Safety ruler*

*Scalpel and cutting board*

*Small hole punch*

*Double-epoxy craft glue*

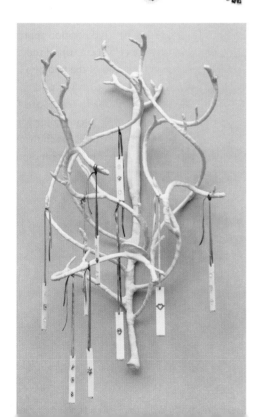

# Raffia Lampshade

**I** Take hold of the wire lampshade frame and, with two strands of raffia, wind the raffia around the frame, starting with the ends of the raffia approximately halfway down on the inside. You will be able to wrap it over two or three times before reaching the end of the raffia. Knot the ends on the inside, keeping a tight tension as you knot. Trim the excess raffia but leave at least ¾ in. (2 cm) to allow any "relaxing" of the strands.

YOU WILL NEED

-------------------------------------------

*Wire "mushroom" coolie lampshade frame, approximately 4 in. (10 cm) in diameter at the top and 12 in. (30 cm) in diameter at the base*

*Long natural raffia, in lengths of 60 in. (150 cm)*

*24 in. (60 cm) burlap (hessian) hat trim*

*Matching sewing thread*

*Needle, scissors*

*Small safety pin (optional)*

-------------------------------------------

**NOTE:** Other sizes or shapes of wire lampshade frames can be used for this project but bear in mind that if you choose one that is too narrow, it will be difficult to knot at the back without the wire gimbal restricting the process.

-------------------------------------------

**SAFETY NOTE:** Only use a low-wattage lamp bulb.

**2** Completely cover the frame with the lengths of raffia with all knots inside the frame.

**3** Cut the hat trim to a length of 20 in. (50 cm) and use to make a bow: fold each end to the center point of the length and stitch together. Turn over and pinch the center into a "pleat," catching with a few stitches to keep in place.

**4** Take the remaining 4 in. (10 cm) of hat trim and fold the raw edges under to make a band about 2 in. (5 cm) wide. Wrap this over the center of the bow and stitch in place at the back. Pin or stitch the bow to the lampshade, at a jaunty angle if you wish! Alternatively, make a bow from silk or a matching ribbon in the same way.

# Diamanté Gift Wraps

**1** For the bow, cut 18 in. (45 cm) of ribbon. Also cut 14 in. (35 cm) of lace at least 3 in. (7 cm) wide, or cut a strip of lace fabric and hem the edges. The lace must be wide enough to overlap the width of the ribbon by at least ½ in. (1 cm) on either side. Position the lace on the ribbon and secure with a few stitches at each short end, gathering in the ends of the lace to neaten and leaving 2 in. (5 cm) of ribbon at each end.

**YOU WILL NEED**

- - - - - - - - - - - - - - - - - - - - - - - - - - - -

*24 in. (60 cm) wired ribbon, 2 in. (5 cm) wide*

*14 in. (35 cm) lace, at least 3 in. (7 cm) wide*

*Matching sewing thread*

*Needle, scissors, pins*

*Diamanté brooch*

*Double-sided sticky tape*

*Short length of diamanté chain*

*Gift tag*

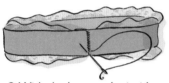

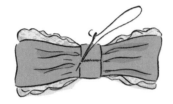

**2** With the lace on the inside, fold each end of the ribbon to the center. Turn one end in by ½ in. (1 cm), overlap the other end by ½ in. (1 cm), and stitch together to secure, using matching sewing thread.

**3** Cut a 5-in. (12-cm) length of ribbon and wrap this around the center of the folded ribbon, to form the bow. Join together at the back over the existing seam. Fold over one end of ribbon by ½ in. (1 cm), overlap the other side by ½ in. (1 cm), and stitch to secure.

**4** Pin a diamanté brooch to the front of the bow. Cut a strip of double-sided tape for the back of the bow and position in place on your wrapped gift. Thread the diamanté chain through the hole in the gift tag and secure with a small piece of tape. Attach the other length of the chain to the wrapped gift with tape.

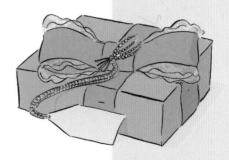

# Floral Linen Runner

**1** This runner will be 95 x 17½ in. (238 x 44 cm), so adapt these measurements to fit your own table. For the base of the runner, cut the linen to 96 x 18½ in. (240 x 46 cm). For the top of the runner, cut two lengths of the vintage floral fabric to 26½ x 18½ in. (66 x 46 cm) and one length of the linen to 44¾ x 18½ in. (112 x 46 cm). With the linen as the central panel, pin the floral fabric to each 18½-in. (46-cm) end, right sides together. Baste (tack) and then machine stitch the pieces together, leaving a ½-in. (1-cm) seam allowance. Press the seams open.

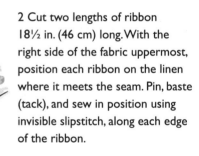

**2** Cut two lengths of ribbon 18½ in. (46 cm) long. With the right side of the fabric uppermost, position each ribbon on the linen where it meets the seam. Pin, baste (tack), and sew in position using invisible slipstitch, along each edge of the ribbon.

**3** Position the top length of runner over the linen base, right sides together, and pin and baste (tack) together. Machine stitch around all four sides, with a ½-in. (1-cm) seam allowance and leaving an opening 8 in. (20 cm) long along one short edge. Trim each corner on the diagonal and press the seams open. Turn the right way out, push out all the corners, and press again. Slipstitch the opening closed.

**4** For the flat bow, cut a length of ribbon
9½ in. (24 cm) long. Fold in both ends to
the middle and stitch in place. For the
center, cut a length of ribbon 3 in. (7 cm) long.
Fold one end under by ½ in. (1 cm), wrap
around the bow, and stitch to secure, at the back.
Repeat this for the second bow. Position the
bows in the middle of the ribbons on the runner
and sew in place.

# Napkins *with* Bow Holders

**1** For a napkin measuring 18½ x 18½ in. (46 x 46 cm), cut a piece of linen that is 20¾ x 20¾ in. (52 x 52 cm). Turn ⅝ in. (1.5 cm) to the wrong side (if there is one) along all four sides, then turn ⅝ in. (1.5 cm) again. Pin and press the folds.

YOU WILL NEED (FOR ONE NAPKIN)

--------------------------------------------

*24 in. (60 cm) linen*

*28 in. (70 cm) grosgrain ribbon, 1 in. (2.5 cm) wide*

*Snap fastener (press stud)*

*Vintage button*

*Matching sewing thread*

*Needle, scissors, pins*

*Sewing machine*

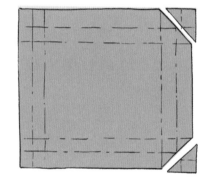

**2** Open out the ironed folds and, with the wrong side facing you, cut across each corner diagonally, approximately 1¼ in. (3 cm) in, across the point where the outer fold lines meet.

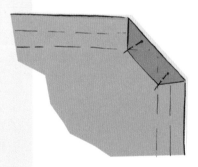

**3** Fold in each corner again, diagonally across the point where the inner fold lines meet. Pin here to hold the fold in place. The fold lines down each side should now all meet up.

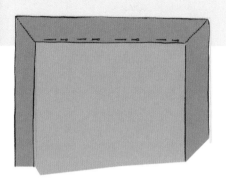

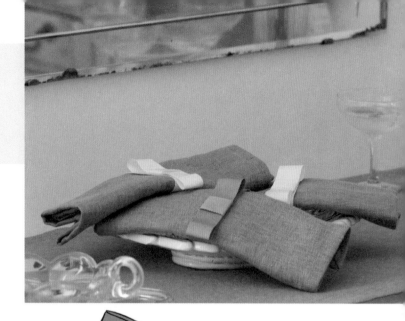

**4** To form the miter, turn in the outer edges at the outer fold, then turn in again at the inner fold. Maneuver the fabric slightly, if necessary, to make sure the mitered point is an exact fit. Pin and baste (tack) the seams in place, then press. Hand stitch the miter closed with invisible slipstitches, then machine stitch around all the seams, close to the folded edge.

**5** For the bow holder, cut a length of ribbon to 13¼ in. (33 cm). With the wrong side facing you, turn under one end by ½ in. (1.3 cm) and again by ⅝ in. (1.5 cm). Hand stitch in place, making sure the stitches do not show on the right side of the ribbon. Repeat at the other end but turn under ½ in. (1.3 cm) and then again by 1½ in. (4 cm). Hand stitch in place as before. Sew a snap fastener (press stud) to each end, and sew a button for decoration onto the right side of the ribbon.

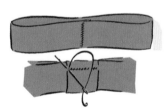

**6** Cut a length of ribbon 8½ in. (21 cm). Fold both ends to the middle point and hand stitch in place. Cut another length of ribbon 3 in. (8 cm), fold under one end by ½ in. (1 cm) and wrap around the "bow" to form the center. Hand stitch in place.

**7** Position the bow on the ribbon and stitch the center part to the holder using tiny invisible stitches.

# Ooh La La Lampshade

1 Lay the scarf wrong side down over the adhesive side of the iron-on backing fabric and iron on, following the maker's instructions. This will protect the scarf if it is frail or damaged and make it easier to handle. Trim away any excess backing fabric, being careful not to cut away the rolled hem edge of the scarf.

2 Position the scarf over the lampshade, wrong side (backing fabric) facing out, aligning the rolled hem edge of the scarf to the bottom of the shade at the front. If there is no rolled edge, allow a ¾-in. (2-cm) overlap at the bottom for a hem. Pin the two sides together where they meet at the back, pulling in the fabric evenly and making sure it fits closely around the shade. Baste (tack) the seam. Trim off the excess fabric around the top of the shade, leaving about 2 in. (5 cm) spare. This will be trimmed again later.

**3** Machine stitch along the basted (tacked) seam, trim away the excess fabric and press the seams open. Turn the fabric right side out and position over the lampshade. Match the rolled hem all around the bottom of the shade, starting about 2½ in. (6 cm) each side of the front where the rolled hem is in exactly the right position and pin up the hem right sides facing, so that the rolled edge is aligned at the bottom. Stitch just underneath the rolled edge, take off the shade, and press the rolled edge down flat over the stitching, then cut away the excess scarf fabric from underneath. Alternatively, hem by turning up the bottom edge by ½ in. (1 cm), then by ½ in. (1 cm) again and hand or machine stitching. This is a better method if the edge of the scarf is damaged or frayed. Pin and tack the Petersham ribbon around the top of the fabric, aligned with the top of the shade. Hand or machine stitch the ribbon in place, overlapping the opposite ends to neaten, and trim away any excess fabric. Flip the Petersham band over so it is on the inside of the shade.

**4** To cover the shade at the back where the scarf doesn't meet up, cut a triangle from the trimmed scarf fabric and pin over the open space, matching up the rolled scarf hem with the existing hem at the bottom of the lampshade. Turn in the edges, pin, and baste (tack) in place. Machine or hand stitch around the edge.

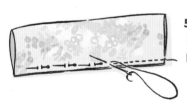

**5** For the bow, cut the remaining scarf to 14 x 7¼ in. (35 x 18 cm). Fold the silk in half lengthwise, wrong sides together, and machine stitch along the three sides with a ½-in. (1-cm) seam allowance and leaving a gap 2¼ in. (6 cm) long in the center of the long edge. Trim away the excess fabric at each corner, turn right way out, push out the corners, and stitch the gap closed. Press flat. Form the bow shape by turning each short end to meet at the back, in the middle. Sew the edges together where they meet. Cut a strip of the remaining scarf 4 x 2 in. (10 x 5 cm) for the center of the bow. Fold in along each long side by ¼ in. (5 mm), then in half again lengthwise. Slipstitch the seam closed and press flat. Gather in, or pleat, the bow at the center and wrap the strip around to meet at the back. Fold over one end by ½ in. (1 cm), overlap the opposite end by ½ in. (1 cm) and stitch to join. Cut the tulle to 20 x 20 in. (50 x 50 cm), gather it up at one corner and stitch to the back of the bow. Stitch the bow and tulle to the back of the lampshade just above the triangular section.

# Daisy Handbag

**1** For the front and back of the bag cut out two squares of felt, each 9¼ x 9¼ in. (23 x 23 cm). Cut out three rectangles, each 5½ x 9¼ in. (14 x 23 cm) for the sides and bottom. Pin and baste (tack) the two side panels to the front and back squares, and then baste (tack) on the base panel, tacking ⅛ in. (3 mm) in from the edge. Using an embroidery or large-eyed needle and all six strands of the stranded embroidery floss (cotton), sew the seams with large running stitches, approximately ¼ in. (5 mm) in from the edge. For the handle, cut a piece of felt to 10 x 1½ in. (25 x 4 cm) and a length of braid to the same size. Pin and baste (tack) the braid over the felt handle then hand stitch in place with tiny stitches along all four sides, staying close to the edges and using matching sewing thread. Pin one end of the handle to the front of the bag on the outside, ¾ in. (2 cm) down from the top edge, then do the same with the handle at the back. Sew in place to secure.

## YOU WILL NEED

-------------------------------------------

*24 x 40 in. (60 x 100 cm) felt*

*Stranded embroidery floss (cotton), to match color of braid or ribbon*

*Embroidery or large-eyed needle*

*1 yd (1 m) braid or wired ribbon, 1½ in. (4 cm) wide*

*Daisy templates on page 141*

*Two glass buttons*

*Matching sewing thread*

*Needle, scissors, pins*

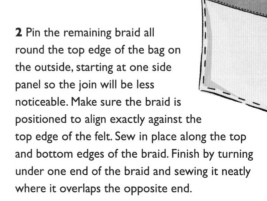

**2** Pin the remaining braid all round the top edge of the bag on the outside, starting at one side panel so the join will be less noticeable. Make sure the braid is positioned to align exactly against the top edge of the felt. Sew in place along the top and bottom edges of the braid. Finish by turning under one end of the braid and sewing it neatly where it overlaps the opposite end.

**3** Use the templates on page 141 to cut out two small daisy shapes 3⅛ in. (8 cm) wide and two large daisy shapes. 4in. (10 cm) wide. Place one large daisy on top of the other and secure with a stitch in the middle. Sew a glass button to the center of the flowers. Repeat with the two smaller daisy shapes. For the bow, cut felt 12 x 1½ in. (30 x 4 cm). Fold in each short end and stitch to join at the back. Cut a smaller piece 2 x ¾ in. (5 x 2 cm) and wrap around the center to form the bow, gathering it in very slightly, and stitch to join at the back. Sew the bow to the braid at the front of the bag and the daisies to the felt.

# Lingerie Envelope

**1** Cut the cotton lining to the same size as your headscarf, in this case 32 x 32 in. (80 x 80 cm), and baste (tack) this to the reverse of the headscarf. This will make the scarf easier to work with, particularly if it is silk, and will stop any show-through of the pattern when the envelope is completed. Cut the silk dupion to the same size and position it over the headscarf, right sides together, and baste (tack) in position. Machine stitch around the edges with a ½-in. (1-cm) seam allowance, leaving a gap of 8 in. (20 cm) along one side. Trim away the excess fabric at the corners and press open the seams. Turn the envelope inside out through the gap, push out the corners, and press. Close up the open section with tiny invisible slipstitches.

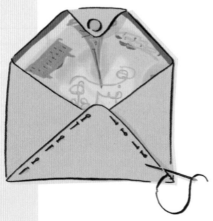

**2** To form the envelope, place the square in front of you with the scarf side facing up and positioned so you are looking at a diamond shape. Fold in the two corners at the sides to meet in the middle and then fold up the bottom corner so that it just overlaps the two triangles. Pin, baste (tack), and hand stitch in place with tiny invisible slipstitches. Fold over the fourth corner to form the envelope flap. Sew a button to the outside, close to the corner point, for decoration. If necessary, you can add a hook-and-eye fastening or snap fastener (press stud) here.

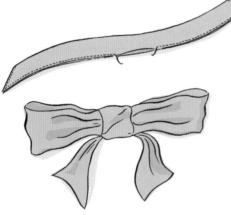

**3** For the bow, cut a length of silk 48 x 4¾ in. (120 x 12 cm). Fold the fabric in half lengthwise, right sides together, and pin along the long edge. Cut each short end at a diagonal so that one side is approximately 2 in. (5 cm) shorter that the other. Machine stitch along the three sides with a ½-in. (1-cm) seam allowance and leaving a gap 4 in. (10 cm) long in the center of the long edge. Cut away any excess fabric from the corners and press open the seams. Turn the right way out, push out the corners, and press again. Hand stitch to close up the open section of seam. Tie into a loose bow and pin or stitch to the outside of the envelope flap.

# Summer Straw Basket

You WILL NEED
--------------------------------------------

*Old straw hat or milliner's straw*

*8 in. (20 cm) broderie anglaise fabric*

*8 in. (20 cm) cotton lining fabric*

*1-in. (2.5-cm) paintbrush*

*Straw stiffener*

*Hat block*

*Thumb tacks (drawing pins)*

*Plastic wrap (cling film)*

*Thin cotton rope or piping cord*

*Pencil (optional)*

*Templates on page 141*

*Matching sewing thread*

*Needle, scissors, pins*

*Sewing machine*

**1** Use the paintbrush to cover the outside of the straw hat with the stiffener, following the manufacturer's instructions. When it is dry and the straw has hardened, dampen down the straw with water to soften it again. Cover the hat block with plastic wrap (clingfilm) to protect it then turn the hat block upside down so that the flat base is uppermost. Pull the straw down firmly over it—you are aiming to stretch the straw so it has a flat base for the bag. As the straw is woven from the middle out, make sure it is centered on the block before pulling or it will be uneven. Use thumb tacks (drawing pins) to hold the straw in place, flat against the block—this will ensure a smooth finish.

**2** When the straw is dry check that the base is completely flat. It can be steam-ironed at this stage if necessary. Remove the straw from the block and turn it right side up. Arrange the sides of the straw into a bag shape. If the straw is a close weave you will need to push holes in the straw to thread the rope through—a pencil is ideal for this. If the straw has an open weave then this won't be necessary. Thread the rope through the straw— you'll need to make six or eight holes at each side of the bag, depending on the number of folds you want.

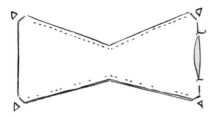

**3** Use the templates on page 141 to cut two large bow shapes to 6 in. (15 cm) wide, one from broderie anglaise and one from the lining fabric. Pin the two fabrics right sides together and machine stitch around the edge about ¼ in. (5 mm) from the edge and leaving a 2½ in. (6 cm) opening along one side. Trim each corner at the diagonal. Turn the bow the right way out by pulling the fabric through the opening, making sure you push out all the corners. Stitch the open edge to close and press flat. For the second smaller bow repeat this step but use the smaller template within the larger one to cut the bow to a width of 5½ in. (14 cm).

**4** Cut a strip of broderie anglaise 2 x 2¾ in. (5 x 7 cm) for the bow center. Fold in each long side by ¼ in. (5 mm) then fold in half lengthwise. Stitch to close the seam. Position the smaller bow on top of the larger bow, with the broderie anglaise side facing, and wrap the strip around the center of the bow, gathering in slightly. Fold one end over at the back by ½ in. (1 cm), overlap the opposite end by ½ in. (1 cm), and sew together to fasten. Sew to the front of the straw bag.

# Needlework Case

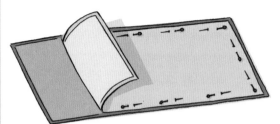

**YOU WILL NEED**

------------------------------------------

*24 in. (60 cm) woolen fabric*

*24 in. (60 cm) lining fabric*

*Cotton ribbon or binding, ½ in. (1 cm) wide*

*Template on page 142*

*Snap fastener (press stud) (optional)*

*Matching sewing threads*

*Needle, scissors, pins*

*Pinking shears*

*Sewing machine*

**1** Cut a piece of woolen fabric 18¾ x 7¾ in. (47 x 19.5 cm). Turn ½ in. (1 cm) to the wrong side along all four edges and pin along the folds. Do the same with the lining fabric, but this time turn ⅝ in. (1.5 cm) to the wrong side. Place the lining fabric on top of the woolen fabric, wrong sides together—you will have about ⅛ in. (2 mm) of wool showing all the way around. Pin the two pieces together and stitch the lining to the wool with invisible slipstitches.

**2** To make the strip, cut a piece of lining fabric 8¼ x 2¼ in. (20.5 x 5.5 cm) and turn ⅝ in. (1.5 cm) to the wrong side along each long side. Press. Cut the ribbon to 8¼ in. (20.5 cm), position over the strip, and machine stitch down both long sides to hide the raw edges.

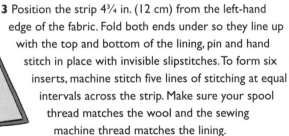

**3** Position the strip 4¾ in. (12 cm) from the left-hand edge of the fabric. Fold both ends under so they line up with the top and bottom of the lining, pin and hand stitch in place with invisible slipstitches. To form six inserts, machine stitch five lines of stitching at equal intervals across the strip. Make sure your spool thread matches the wool and the sewing machine thread matches the lining.

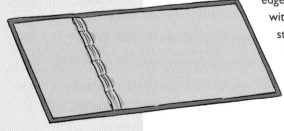

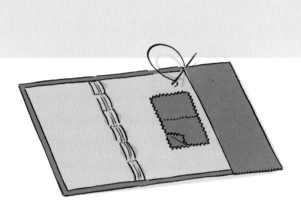

**4** Use the pinking shears to cut two rectangles of wool, each 2¾ x 4 in. (7 x 10 cm). With right sides uppermost, lay one on top of the other and position in the center of the fabric piece. Pin and machine stitch across the center. To form the pocket, fold the right-hand edge of the fabric piece over by 3 in. (7 cm), pin and hand stitch the two sides together with invisible slipstitch.

**5** To form the bow, use the template on page 142 to cut two bow shapes to 6¾ in. (17 cm) wide, one from the woolen fabric and one from the lining material. Fold the raw edges to the wrong side by ¼ in. (7 mm) and press. Place the pieces on top of each other, wrong sides together, pin and hand stitch with invisible slipstitch (do this from lining side). With the wool side facing you, pinch the center to form a little pleat and catch with a few stitches. Cut a piece of woolen fabric 3 x 1¾ in. (8 x 4.7 cm), and turn the long edges to the wrong side so your strip is about ¾ in. (2 cm) wide and slipstitch down the seam.

**6** To finish the needlework case, fold it twice, starting from the right, so that the remaining part becomes the front flap. Loop the strip of wool around the bow and catch with a few stitches at the back to secure. Position the bow centrally on the front flap and stitch the loop to the wool, taking care not to go through to the lining behind. Finally, add a snap fastener (press stud) here if you wish.

# Bow Belle Frames

**1** First choose a beautiful image from a vintage magazine and find a suitably sized frame for it. If necessary, remove any old paint or varnish from the frame and paint it in your chosen color. Using the scalpel, ruler, and cutting board, cut the polyboard to fit neatly within the back of the frame and cut the watercolor paper to the same size. Take your vintage magazine image and glue it to the watercolor paper—use spray adhesive, because you will get a good even coverage and you can peel off and reposition the image if necessary. Slip the paper, backed by the polyboard, into the picture frame and, following the manufacturer's instructions, use a picture framing kit to secure.

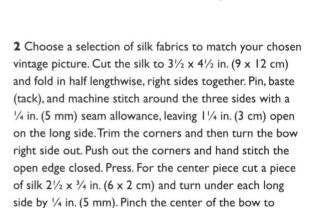

## You will need

-------------------------------------------

*Vintage picture frame*

*Vintage magazine image*

*Silk fabric in assorted colors, 4 in. (10 cm) for each bow*

*Sheet polyboard*

*Sheet 140-lb (300-gsm) watercolor paper*

*Spray adhesive*

*Picture framing kit (optional)*

*Scalpel and cutting board*

*Ruler*

*Needle, scissors, pins*

*Matching sewing thread*

*Multipurpose glue suitable for wood and silk*

**2** Choose a selection of silk fabrics to match your chosen vintage picture. Cut the silk to 3½ x 4½ in. (9 x 12 cm) and fold in half lengthwise, right sides together. Pin, baste (tack), and machine stitch around the three sides with a ¼ in. (5 mm) seam allowance, leaving 1¼ in. (3 cm) open on the long side. Trim the corners and then turn the bow right side out. Push out the corners and hand stitch the open edge closed. Press. For the center piece cut a piece of silk 2½ x ¾ in. (6 x 2 cm) and turn under each long side by ¼ in. (5 mm). Pinch the center of the bow to gather and then wrap the center piece around it. Turn under one short end at the back, overlap the opposite end and then stitch together to secure. Plump out the bow slightly, then add a spot of glue to the back and glue to the picture frame. Add as many colored bows as you wish, in colors to match your image.

# Teatime Tablecloth

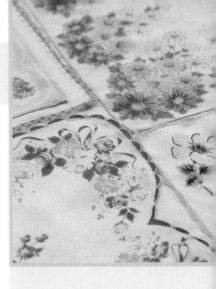

**1** Position the handkerchiefs in a square, making sure you are happy with the arrangement, and measure the overall area. Cut out the voile to this measurement, adding an extra ¾ in. (2 cm) all around for the hem. Turn the voile under by ½ in. (1 cm) and again by another ½ in. (1 cm). Pin and hem with an invisible slipstitch. You may want to cut the corners diagonally to avoid less bulk. Press.

**2** Arrange the handkerchiefs in position on top of the voile and pin in place. Hand stitch each one onto the top of the voile with invisible slipstitches. Where the handkerchiefs overlap the edge of the voile, particularly if one of them has a scalloped edge, turn the tablecloth over and slipstitch the voile to the handkerchiefs.

**3** Measure approximately 3½ in. (9 cm) diagonally in from each corner and mark the position. Fold each length of ribbon in half and hand stitch along the fold at each of these four points. Tie the ribbons in bows, letting the ribbon ends trail down.

**YOU WILL NEED**

-------------------------------------

*Four vintage floral handkerchiefs*

*Cotton voile, approximately 24 x 24 in. (60 x 60 cm)*

*Four 1-yd (1-m) lengths of rayon ribbon in assorted colors*

*Matching sewing thread*

*Needle, scissors, pins*

-------------------------------------

**NOTE:** Four 12-in. (30-cm) square handkerchiefs will make a 24-in. (60-cm) square tablecloth—perfect for a little café table.

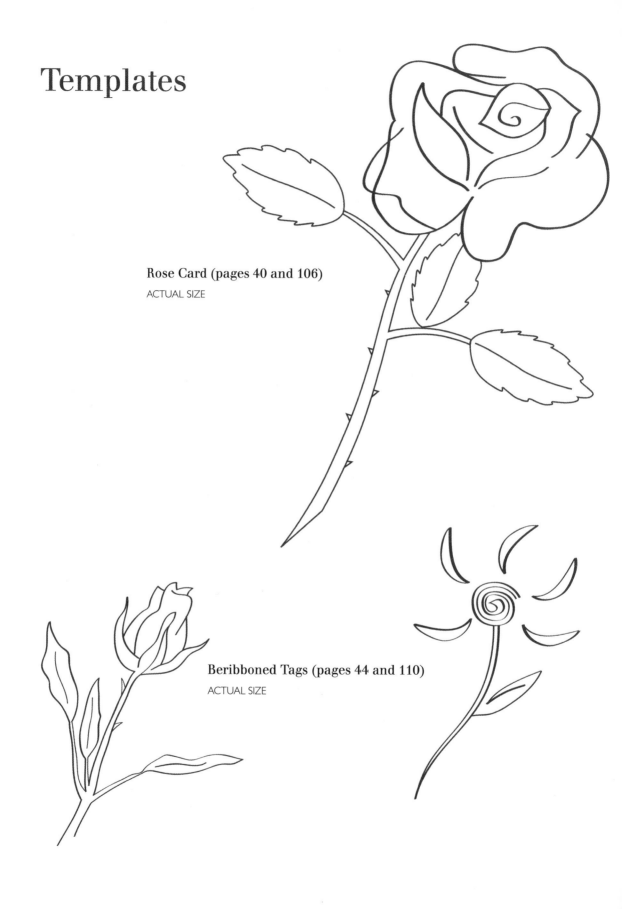

# Templates

**Rose Card (pages 40 and 106)**
ACTUAL SIZE

**Beribboned Tags (pages 44 and 110)**
ACTUAL SIZE

Daisy Handbag (pages 74 and 130)

ACTUAL SIZE

Summer Straw Basket (pages 76 and 134) ACTUAL SIZE

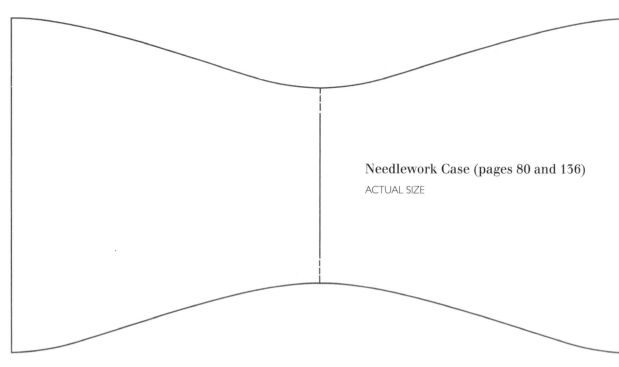

Needlework Case (pages 80 and 136)
ACTUAL SIZE

# Resources

## UK

**ANTIQUES NEWS**
www.antiquesnews.co.uk
Internet newspaper for antiques news and fairs

**THE BAG 'N' BOX MAN**
Tel: 01295 788522
www.bagnboxman.co.uk
Supplier of raffia, bags, and boxes

**BERMONDSEY SQUARE ANTIQUES MARKET**
Fridays 4am-2pm
www.bermondseysquare.co.uk

**BOROVICK FABRICS**
Tel: 020 7437 2180
www.borovickfabricsltd.co.uk
Wide range of fabrics and silks

**THE BUTTON LADY**
Tel: 020 7435 5412
www.buttonladyhampstead.co.uk
Antique buttons and buckles

**CAMDEN PASSAGE MARKET**
www.camdenpassageislington.co.uk
Antiques and bric-à-brac market

**JJ CASH LABELS**
Tel: 024 7646 6466
www.jjcash.co.uk
Woven clothing labels and nametapes

**CLOTH HOUSE**
Tel: 020 7437 5155 and
Tel: 020 7287 1555
London W1F 0QJ
www.clothhouse.com
Fabrics, vintage buttons, and braids

**DESIGNERS GUILD**
Tel (Head Office): 020 7893 7400
www.designersguild.com
Furnishing fabrics, wallpapers, and linens, including the Brera Alta linen used for Floral Linen Runner (page 68) and Napkins with Bow Holders (page 70)

**DONNA FLOWER**
Tel: 07896 922694
www.donnaflower.com
Antique, vintage, and retro fabrics

**GREEN & STONE OF CHELSEA**
Tel: 020 7352 0837
www.greenandstone.com
Art supplies

**JOHN LEWIS**
Tel: 020 7629 7711
www.johnlewis.com
Department stores

**LOVED AGAIN**
Tel: Monica Rivron 07798 802925
Email: monica.rivron@mac.com
Vintage kitchenalia, linens, handkerchiefs, and doilies

**LUNN ANTIQUES**
Tel: 020 7736 4638
www.lunnantiques.com
Antique lace and textiles

**M AND F PRODUCTS**
Tel: 01424 844416
Lampshade frames and ring sets

**MACCULLOCH AND WALLIS**
Tel: 020 7629 0311
www.macculloch-wallis.co.uk
Haberdashery, trimmings, millinery straws and stiffeners

MAUD AND MABEL
Tel: 07956 851549
www.maudandmabel.com
Unique pieces and gifts, contemporary
and vintage ceramics, textiles and glass

MISAN TEXTILES
Tel: 020 7734 5441
www.misan.co.uk
Silk, cotton, jersey, and woollen fabrics

MOON DOLL BOUTIQUE
Tel: 07950 233680
www.moondoll.co.uk
Vintage scarves

PAPERCHASE
Tel: 020 7467 6200
www.paperchase.co.uk
Art materials and different papers

PORTOBELLO ROAD MARKET
www.portobellomarket.org
World famous antiques market

RETROSTUFF
Tel: 07876 748595
www.retrostuff-etc.com
www.etsy.com/shop/tinselandtatters
Vintage lace, trimmings, and beadwork

VV ROULEAUX
Tel: 020 7224 5179
www.vvrouleaux.com
Ribbons, trims, braids, and flowers

THE SILK SOCIETY
Tel: 020 7287 1881
www.thesilksociety.com
Large range of luxurious fabrics

SUNBURY ANTIQUE MARKET,
Tel: 01932 230946
www.sunburyantiques.com
Antique market with 700 stalls inside
and out

DIANE JULIE WRIGHT
Email: knightdiane@ymail.com
Vintage jewellery and accessories

# NORTH AMERICA

ANTIQUE 67
www.antique67.com
Canada's antiques fairs listings directory

ANTIQUE TRADER
www.antiquetrader.com
Antique fairs and flea market listings

ART SHACK
www.artshack.ca
Art supplies and materials

BRITEX FABRICS
Tel: +1 (415) 392-2910
www.britexfabrics.com
Fabrics, ribbon, buttons, and lace

DOLLS AND LACE
www.dollsandlace.com
Vintage silk flowers, lace, and millinery

DRESS IT UP
www.jessejamesbeads.com
Buttons and embellishments.

FABRIC LAND
www.fabricland.ca
Large selection of fabrics with stores
across Canada

HANCOCK'S
Tel: +1 (800) 845-8723
www.hancocks-paducah.com
Fabrics and notions

JOANN'S
Tel: +1 (888) 739-4120
www.joann.com
Fabrics and haberdashery with stores
across the US

MICHAEL'S
Tel: +1 (800) 642-4235
www.michaels.com
Arts and crafts supplier with stores
across the US and Canada

RENAISSANCE RIBBONS
Tel: +1 (887) 422-6601
www.renaissanceribbons.com
Supplier of woven ribbons and trims

REX ART
Tel: +1 (800) 739-2782
www.rexart.com
Art supplies and materials

TIMELESS TRIMS
Tel: +1 (887) 422-6601
www.timelesstrims.com
Vintage trims and fabrics

# Index

curtains
filigree curtain 20–21, 96
handkerchief café curtain 32–33, 103
lace and ribbon tie-backs 30–31, 102
cushions
blossom and fern tie cushion 52–53,
116–117
embellished silk cushions 12–13, 88–89
silk and lace bolster 14–15, 90–91

**D**
diamanté trinkets
à la mode cards 58–59, 120
diamanté gift wraps 66–67, 123
diamanté pendants 60–61, 121
jeweled mirror 48–49, 113
lace jewelry roll 28–29, 100–101
silk satin pouches 16–17, 92–93
doilies and placemats
doily corsage napkins 24–25, 98
embellished silk cushions 12–13, 88–89
filigree curtain 20–21, 96
silk satin pouches 16–17, 92–93

**E**
envelopes
handkerchief envelopes 34–35, 104
lingerie envelope 78–79, 132–133

**F**
fabrics, vintage
floral linen runner 68–69, 124–125
vintage drawstring bags 50–51,
114–115
felt: daisy handbag 74–75, 130–131
frames
bow belle frames 82–83, 138
rosette frame 56–57, 119

**G**
gift bags, tissue and lace 26–27, 99

gift tags
beribboned tags 44–45, 110–111
diamanté pendants 60–61, 121
gift wraps, diamanté 66–67, 123
grosgrain ribbon 70

**H**
handkerchiefs
embellished silk cushions 12–13, 88–89
handkerchief café curtain 32–33, 103
handkerchief envelopes 34–35, 104
teatime tablecloth 84–85, 139

**J**
Jewelry roll 28–29, 100–101

**L**
lampshades
frou-frou lampshade 18–19, 94–95
ooh la la lampshade 72–73, 128–129
raffia lampshade 62–63, 122
lingerie envelope 78–79, 132–133

**M**
magazine illustrations
à la mode cards 58–59, 120
bow belle frames 82–83, 138
rosette frame 56–57, 119
mirror, jeweled 48–49

**N**
napkins
doily corsage napkins 24–25, 98
napkins with bow holders 70–71,
126–127
needlework case 80–81, 136–137
notebook 36–37, 105

**P**
Petersham ribbon 70

pouches and rolls
lace jewelry roll 28–29, 100–101
lingerie envelope 78–79, 132–133
needlework case 80–81, 136–137
silk satin pouches 16–17

**R**
raffia lampshade 64–65, 122

**S**
scarves
blossom and fern tie cushion 52–53,
116–117
lingerie envelope 78–79, 132–133
ooh la la lampshade 72–73, 128–129
vintage scarf chairbacks 46–47, 112
silk and silk dupion
embellished silk cushions 12–13, 88–89
frou-frou lampshade 18–19, 94–95
lace jewelry roll 28–29, 100–101
lingerie envelope 78–79, 132–133
silk and lace bolster 14–15, 90–91
silk satin pouches 16–17, 92–93
silk, ironing 92, 112

**T**
table runners
floral linen runner 68–69, 124–125
lace and Burmese cotton runner
22–23, 97
teatime tablecloth 84–85, 139
templates 140–142

**V**
velvet ribbon throw 54–55, 118

**W**
wool
needlework case 80–81, 136–137
velvet ribbon throw 54–55, 118

## Acknowledgments

We wish to thank everyone who helped in the making of this book, especially
Cindy, Sally, Clare and Penny at Cico, Caroline, our photographer, the owners of
the location houses, the close friends who kindly lent items from their personal
vintage collections, and of course, the stall holders we met along the way!